AGRIPPA'S BUILDING ACTIVITIES IN ROME

AGRIPPA'S BUILDING ACTIVITIES IN ROME

BY

FREDERICK W. SHIPLEY

PROFESSOR OF LATIN

WASHINGTON UNIVERSITY

WIPF & STOCK · Eugene, Oregon

Wipf and Stock Publishers
199 W 8th Ave, Suite 3
Eugene, OR 97401

Agrippa's Building Activities in Rome
By Shipley, Frederick W.
ISBN 13: 978-1-60608-244-7
Publication date 11/21/2008
Previously published by Washington University, 1933

PREFACE

THE present paper is the second of a series of articles dealing with the rebuilding of Rome in the period from the death of Caesar to the death of Augustus. The first was published in the *Memoirs of the American Academy in Rome,* Vol. IX, 1931. In addition to a chronological summary for the entire period, based upon inscriptions and ancient authors, it contained a chapter on the building operations of the *Triumphales,* exclusive of Augustus, pp. 9-44. This second paper deals with the building operations of Agrippa, who, though more deserving of a triumph than any of the *Triumphales* whose buildings are recorded in the previous chapter, persistently declined that honor. With the single exception of Augustus himself, Agrippa is more entitled to the credit of changing the Rome of the Republic into the imperial city than is any Roman of the period. In Regions IX and VII, the plain which lay between the hills (the Pincian, the Esquiline, and the Capitoline) and the Tiber, his building operations were even more significant than those of Augustus himself.

Much of the area covered by the structures of Agrippa was swept by the fire of Titus, and the more important buildings underwent wholesale reconstruction, notably by Hadrian. The scanty, and sometimes conflicting, evidence of the ancient authors can therefore be supplemented only by equally scant archaeological evidence dating from the time of Agrippa himself. Future excavations, especially in the Campus Martius, may add much to our knowledge of Agrippa's actual work. In the meantime I have done what I could *pro parte mea,* with the evidence thus far available, to recover what can be gleaned from our present sources of information in regard to the building activities of this self-effacing man, who not only played an important part in the building of the Empire itself, but also in the building of the new Rome of the time of Augustus.

I am indebted to Dr. Axel Boethius of the Swedish Archaeological Institute in Rome, who on his recent visit to the United States patiently listened to the reading of this study, for many valuable criticisms. He is not responsible for any of its errors. I also desire to make grateful acknowledgment to my former teacher in the field of Roman topography, Dr. Christian Huelsen, whose various articles, particularly those dealing with the Campus Martius, have laid the foundation for much of the material contained in this study. Though no longer active in this particular field, his work as pioneer must always be reckoned with.

I am also indebted to Professor Huelsen for the kind permission to reprint the plans which appear in Figs. 1 and 2 and to Dr. Armin von Gerkan for a similar courtesy in allowing me to reproduce his ground plan of the Pantheon in Fig. 3. The map given in Fig. 4 is necessarily a sketch, indicating merely the location of Agrippa's structures, since in most cases we lack the details necessary for a complete ground plan of the buildings as they stood in Agrippa's day. With regard to the Diribitorium, the Basilica Neptuni and the Sepulcrum Agrippae, we are not even sure of their exact location.

All citations from ancient authors as well as from inscriptions are given in the footnotes. Where the passage is important the text is given in full. The text of certain passages has been given in the Appendix, either because of their length, or because of the frequency of reference. For reasons of economy in type-setting, as well as consideration for the appearance of the page, passages from the Greek have been given in translation *(Loeb Library)* in the body of the text, but where the passage is important, or frequently referred to, the Greek text has been printed in the Appendix.

Where modern authorities are cited but once the full bibliographical reference is given in the footnotes. Where a work is cited frequently I have resorted to abbreviated titles, a key to which immediately follows the table of contents.

FREDERICK W. SHIPLEY.

Washington University, St. Louis, Mo.
August 14, 1933.

TABLE OF CONTENTS

KEY TO ABBREVIATED TITLES USED IN BIBLIOGRAPHICAL REFERENCES

Full titles of books and articles, cited but once or rarely, are given in the footnotes.[1] Abbreviated titles used for works frequenly cited, and particularly for standard works and scientific periodicals are given in full below.

Acque = R. Lanciani, *I commentarii di Frontino intorno le acque e gli acquedotti.* Rome, Salviucci, 1880.

Anderson, Spiers, Ashby = *The Architecture of Ancient Rome.* London, 1927.

Athenaeum = *Athenaeum, Studii Periodici di Letteratura e Storia dell' Antichità.* Regia Università, Pavia.

BMC = *British Museum Catalogue of Coins of the Roman Empire,* Vol. I. London, 1924.

Bull. Com. = *Bulletino della Commissione Archeologica Comunale di Roma.* Rome, 1872—.

Bull. Inst. = *Bulletino dell' Instituto di Corrispondenza Archeologica.* Rome, 1829-1885.

CIL = *Corpus Inscriptionum Latinarum.* Berlin, 1863—.

Class. Mon. = G. Lugli, *The Classical Monuments of Rome and Its Vicinity,* translated by G. Bagnani. Rome, 1928.

Curiosum = *Curiosum Urbis Romae Regionum XIV cum Breviariis suis.* This is one form of the so-called Regionary Catalogue (the *Notitia* being the other). *App.* following Curiosum refers to its Appendix.

Dar. Saglio = Daremberg et Saglio, *Dictionnaire des Antiquités.* Paris, 1887-1919.

Eph. Epig. = *Ephemeris Epigraphica.* Berlin, 1872—.

Eranos = *Eranos, Acta Philologica Suecana.* Goteburg, 1903—.

FUR = *Forma Urbis Romae Regionum XIV.* Ed. Jordan. Berlin, 1874.

Gnomon = *Gnomon, Kritische Zeitschrift für die Gesamte Klassische Altertumswissenschaft.* Berlin, 1924—.

Jour. Rom. Stud. = *Journal of Roman Studies.* London, 1911—.

Klio = *Klio, Beiträge zur alten Geschichte.* Leipzig, 1907—.

Lugli = See under *Class. Mon.*

Mem. Am. Acad. = *Memoirs of the American Academy in Rome* (Vol. IX). Rome, 1917—.

[1] Absence of reference in the bibliographical notes to the excellent dissertation of Meyer Reinhold entitled *Marcus Agrippa, a Biography,* is due to the fact that this recent study appeared after the present article was already in page proof.

Mitt. = *Mittheilungen des Deutschen Archäologischen Instituts, Römische Abtheilung.* Rome, 1886—.

Mon. Antich. = *Monumenti Antichi pubblicati per cura della R. Accademia dei Lincei.* Milan, 1890—.

Mon. Germ. Hist. = *Monumenta Germaniae Historica Auctorum Antiquissimorum,* Vol. IX. Berlin, 1892.

Notitia = See under *Curiosum.*

Not. Scav. = *Notizie degli Scavi di Antichità communicate alla R. Accademia dei Lincei.* Rome, 1876—.

Paully-Wissowa = *Realencyclopädie des Klassischen Altertums.* Stuttgart, 1894—.

Platner-Ashby = *A Topographical Dictionary of Ancient Rome,* by Samuel Ball Platner, completed and revised by Thomas Ashby. London, 1929.

R. and E. = R. Lanciani, *The Ruins and Excavations of Ancient Rome.* London and New York, 1898.

Rom. Build. Rep. = Tenney Frank, *Roman Buildings of the Republic* (*Papers of the American Academy in Rome,* No. iii). Rome, 1924.

Rosch. = Roscher, *Lexicon der griechischen und römischen Mythologie.* Leipzig, 1884—.

Top. = *Topographie der Stadt Rom in Altertum.* Vol. I, Parts 1, 2 and Vol. II are by H. Jordan, Berlin, 1871-1875. Vol. I, Part 3 (referred to in notes as I^3) is by Ch. Hülsen, Berlin, 1906.

Top. Dict. = See Platner-Ashby.

Year's Work = *The Year's Work in Classical Studies.* London, 1908—.

INTRODUCTION

In the first of a series of chapters on the building operations in Rome from the death of Caesar to the death of Augustus, I dealt with the commemorative buildings erected by the numerous generals who celebrated triumphs during this period.[1] Some of these generals played relatively unimportant rôles, and in the case of several of them history has left us in ignorance as to the victories for which the triumphs were awarded. The triumphs in certain cases seem to have been in the nature of political rewards granted by Octavian and Antony as they jockeyed for position in the struggle for the hegemony of the Roman world.

The one outstanding general of the period from 44 to 12 B. C. was Agrippa, who towers like a colossus above these smaller figures. He possessed the military genius, at least in the field, which Octavian himself lacked. Had it not been for Agrippa, it is very doubtful whether the prestige of the young Caesar would have survived the disasters in the campaign with Sextus Pompey, and the subsequent history of the Roman Empire might have been quite different.

The catalogue of his military services is a long and distinguished one: his part in the Perusian War in 41/40 B. C.; his operations against Sextus Pompey and his defeat of part of Antony's forces at Sipontum in 40; his campaigns against the rebellious Gauls which ended victoriously in 37, involving the crossing of the Rhine and the subjugation of Aquitania; his building of a fleet in 37 in the naval base which he constructed in the Lucrine Lake, and his two victories at Mylae and Naulochus in 36 which put an end to Pompey's power in Sicily; his campaign against the Dalmatians in 34; his naval victories in the campaign which ended at Actium in 31; his subjugation of the Cantabrians in 19; the quelling of the revolt of the tribes of

[1] *Memoirs of the American Academy in Rome,* IX, 9-44.

the Cimmerian Bosphorus in 14; and his suppression in 13 B. C., shortly before his death, of the revolt of the Pannonians. Any one of the services here recounted was as significant as any of the military exploits of the *triumphales* recorded in the previous article; many of them were much more significant than those of some of the *triumphales* in the list who, as Dio[2] says, celebrated triumphs "merely for arresting robbers, or for restoring harmony to cities torn by factional strife."

But Agrippa consistently refused to accept a triumph, although we have record of three which were voted him by the Senate at the request of Augustus. The first of these occasions was in 37 B. C., the year of his first consulship, when Octavian recalled Agrippa from Gaul to aid in the war with Sextus Pompey in which he himself had fared so badly in the preceding year. According to Dio,[3] "He had sent for this man, who had been fighting against the insurgent Gauls at the time when he had been the second of the Romans to cross the Rhine for war, and after honoring him by the bestowal of a triumph he bade him finish the work on the fleet and train the men. Agrippa who was consul with Lucius Gallus did not celebrate his triumph, considering it disgraceful for him to make a display when Caesar had fared so poorly, but set to work with enthusiasm to fit out the fleet." The second occasion was in 19 B. C. when Agrippa put down an uprising of the Cantabrians in Spain, and forced them to live in the plains.[4] Agrippa declined the triumph offered him, although in this very year Cornelius Balbus, another of the generals of Augustus, celebrated a triumph *ex Africa,* and built a theatre to commemorate it.[5] In 14 B. C. a triumph was voted him for the third

[2] Dio LIV, 12.

[3] Dio XLVIII, 49, 3. (*Loeb. Lib.* translations have been used in all translations from the Greek.)

[4] Dio LIV, 11, who goes on to say "yet he sent no communication concerning them to the Senate, and did not accept a triumph, although one was voted him at the behest of Augustus, but showed moderation in these matters as was his wont."

[5] See *Mem. Am. Acad. in Rome,* IX, p. 37 sq. It was in connection with the declining of this triumph that Dio (LIV, 12) makes the remarks which I have cited above (n. 2).

time for quelling a revolt of the tribes of the Cimmerian Bosphorus. Agrippa did not even take the trouble to notify the Senate of what he had accomplished and again declined the celebration of a triumph.[6]

This is not the place to discuss in detail Agrippa's motives in thus declining the triumphs offered him. Dio has stated, in regard to the first, that he did not wish to embarrass Octavian by celebrating a triumph when the latter was suffering from a series of reverses. The other two occasions were not comparable in importance with Agrippa's two great naval achievements in Sicily and at Actium for which Octavian as Commander-in-Chief celebrated respectively an ovation and a triumph, although he awarded to his victorious admiral certain exceptional honors.[7] Agrippa's refusal of triumphs for himself may have been due to a fixed policy of strengthening the hand of his superior by giving him all the credit. But one suspects, along with it, a touch of a certain kind of pride, not exactly "the pride which apes humility," but still a pride which led him to let his own achievements speak for themselves, and by declining the honors which fell to the lot of lesser men, he placed his own military services in a class apart. The man who chose to step back into the aedileship after having held the consulship was something of a paradox, who either weighed honors lightly, or sincerely felt that the highest honor was the consciousness of a task well done.

But while Agrippa steadfastly declined triumphs, he outdid

[6] Dio LIV, 25. Dio adds, as his own opinion, that because Agrippa declined to celebrate a triumph no one else of his peers was permitted to do so any longer, but they enjoyed merely the distinction of triumphal honors.

[7] There is an interesting statement in Dio LI, 21, in regard to Octavian's triple triumph: "As for the triumph, Caesar celebrated on the first day his victories over the Pannonians and Dalmatians, the Iapydes and their neighbors, and some Germans and Gauls. For Gaius Carrinas had subdued the Morini and others who had revolted with them, and had repulsed the Suebi, who had crossed the Rhine to wage war. Not only did Carrinas, therefore, celebrate the triumph . . . but Caesar also celebrated it, since the credit of the victory properly belonged to his position as supreme commander." Carrinas actually celebrated his triumph on July 14, 28 B. C. If Octavian conceded a triumph to an obscure general like Carrinas, it is more than likely that he offered Agrippa a triumph for the Actian campaign, though of this we have no record.

all the *triumphales* of the period, excepting Augustus himself, in the erection of public buildings. The erection of a public building from the spoils of war to commemorate a triumph was one of the prerogatives of a *triumphalis*. Agrippa built many buildings, one at least, the Basilica Neptuni, to commemorate his naval victories. As he came of an obscure, and probably not a wealthy family,[8] the millions which he spent upon buildings and public works presumably came from the *manubiae*, as in the case of the *triumphales*. We may assume that Augustus compensated him for his modesty in declining the actual triumph by seeing to it that the *manubiae* for his building operations were ample. The man who chose to build sewers which few people could see, and aqueducts which were likewise mostly underground, was likely to be favored in the matter of funds for these modest and unostentatious undertakings, as he was also favored later when, after the battle of Actium, he was engaged upon the monumental structures of the Campus Martius. At this period Augustus was exerting pressure upon the *triumphales* to build roads,[9] and we know that Messalla, Calvisius and indeed Augustus himself were engaged in this work during the years 28 and 27 B. C.[10] But an exception was made in the case of Agrippa, who had already performed in a notable manner his share in such utilitarian undertakings, and he was allowed, or rather encouraged, to proceed with the complex of buildings enumerated in Group II, without jealousy, as Dio[11] says, on the part of Augustus.

The building activities of Agrippa may be discussed most conveniently under four groups. The first of these embraces his utilitarian activities pertaining for the most part to his aedileship in 33 B. C.; the second and third are arranged topographically, the former dealing with his constructions in

[8] About the year 40 B. C. he married his first wife, Pomponia, the daughter of Atticus, who, by reason of her father's wealth, may have brought him a considerable dowry.

[9] Dio LIII, 22, 2; 23, 2; Suet. *Aug.* 30.

[10] *Mem. Am. Acad. in Rome*, IX, 33-36.

[11] LIII, 23, 2.

Region IX, and the latter dealing with those in Region VII; the fourth is a miscellaneous group, comprising his known activities in Regions VIII and XI.

These four groups are as follows:

(1) The works of his aedileship, and particularly the sewers and aqueducts, though the latter continued to be his special province until his death in 12 B. C., when Augustus himself took over his work.

(2) His building activities in that part of the Campus Martius between the Via Flaminia and the river, which became Region IX of Augustus, including the Saepta, the Diribitorium, the Basilica Neptuni and Porticus Argonautarum, the Pantheon, the Laconicum Sudatorium, the Thermae, the Stagnum Agrippae, the Horti, the Euripus and the Pons Agrippae.

(3) His building activities in the Campus Martius east of the Via Flaminia, in what became Region VII of Augustus, namely, the Campus Agrippae and the Porticus Vipsania (containing Agrippa's famous map) built by his sister after his death, and according to his plans.

(4) The Horrea Agrippiana, and the Hydra fountain figure in Region VIII, and the dolphins and *ova* on the spina of the Circus in Region XI.

But before discussing these groups it will be convenient to give in tabular form the chronological data (sometimes conflicting) furnished by the ancient sources.

Chronological Data From Ancient Sources Concerning the Building Operations of Agrippa

40 B. C. According to Dio XLVIII, 32, 3, Agrippa (who was praetor in this year) brought the Aqua Julia to Rome. Frontinus, *de Aquis,* I, 9, places this event in Agrippa's aedileship, 33 B. C.

34 B. C. Dio XLIX, 42, 2, places the repair of the Aqua Marcia in this year. Frontinus, *de Aquis,* I, 9, puts it in 33 B. C., the year of Agrippa's aedileship.

33 B. C. Agrippa becomes aedile, four years after his consulship, and is credited with the following public works:

1. Without charge to the public treasury he repaired all the public buildings, all the streets, and cleaned out the sewers, passing through them by boat into the Tiber (Dio XLIX, 43, 1; Plin., *N. H.*, XXXVI, 15, 104).

2. He built the Aqua Julia and added to the Tepula (Frontinus, *de Aquis*, I, 9). According to Dio XLVIII, 32, 3, the building of the Julia is placed in 40 B. C.

Plin., *N. H.*, XXXVI, 121, erroneously ascribes the building of the Aqua Virgo to this year. Dio and Frontinus agree in placing it in 19 B. C., giving the consuls.

3. According to Frontinus, *de Aquis*, I, 9, he repaired the following aqueducts: Appia, Anio Vetus, and Marcia. (Dio placed the repair of the Marcia in 34 B. C.)

4. He adorned the city with ornamental fountains (Plin., *N. H.*, XXXVI, 121). The hydra with which Festus (290) says Agrippa adorned the Lacus Servilius was probably one of these.

5. He placed on the *spina* of the circus dolphins and egg-shaped markers to indicate the laps in the races (Dio XLIX, 43, 2).

26 B. C. He dedicated the Saepta Julia in the Campus Martius. This had been begun by Julius Caesar and his work had been continued by Lepidus. Agrippa had adorned it with marble tablets and paintings (Cic. *Att.*, IV, 16, 14; Dio LIII, 32, 1).

25 B. C. Agrippa in this year completes the following units of his extensive building program in the Campus Martius:

1. The Porticus Argonautarum (ἡ στοὰ τοῦ Ποσειδῶνος) in commemoration of his naval victories (Dio LIII, 27, 1; *Schol. Iuven.*, VI, 154).

2. The Laconicum Sudatorium (τὸ πυρατήριον τὸ Λακωνικὸν) Dio LIII, 27, 1.

3. Dio LIII, 27, 2, dates the completion of the Pantheon in this year. The inscription, *CIL*, VI, 896, has *COS·TERTIUM*, which may mean any time after Jan. 1, 27 B. C. (See pp. 56, 57.)

19 B. C. Agrippa brings the Aqua Virgo into the city at his own expense, and dedicates it June 9 (Frontinus, *de Aquis*, I, 10; Dio LIV, 11, 7). Pliny, *N. H.*, XXXVI, 121, erroneously dates this event in 33 B. C., the aedileship of Agrippa.

With the construction of the Aqua Virgo we should probably associate also the Thermae Agrippae, the Stagnum, the Euripus, the Horti Agrippae, and possibly a temple of Bonus Eventus.

12 B. C. Agrippa died late in March leaving to the Roman people his Gardens and Baths, with provision for maintenance (Dio LIV, 28; 29, 4).

The following buildings concerning which we have no datable evidence had been presumably completed: the Pons Agrippae, the Horrea Agrippiana, and Agrippa's tomb in the Campus Martius (though he was not buried there, but in the Mausoleum of Augustus).

Dio LV, 8, 3, 5, states that the Diribitorium was not completed until 7 B. C., five years after Agrippa's death, and that the Porticus Vipsania (which contained Agrippa's map) was still unfinished in that year. We have no datable information concerning the Campus Agrippae upon which the Porticus Vipsania stood.

GROUP I

AGRIPPA'S PUBLIC WORKS AS AEDILE—THE SEWERS AND AQUEDUCTS

Group I

AGRIPPA'S PUBLIC WORKS AS AEDILE—THE SEWERS AND AQUEDUCTS

We are not informed what the reasons were which induced Agrippa to assume the aedileship in the year 33 B. C. He had already held the praetorship in 40, and the consulship in 37. His willingness to assume an office lower down in the *cursus honorum* was the subject of comment by the ancient authorities, but they give no inkling of the purpose which lay behind this unusual step. But Agrippa was no ordinary man, as is shown by his consistent refusal to accept the triumphs awarded him. We can only venture guesses at his motives. We may assume at once that his purpose was constructive and not actuated by personal ambition. While numerous *triumphales,* partisans of Antony as well as of Octavian, were erecting the buildings recorded in the previous paper[1] in commemoration of their triumphs, it is more than likely that the public buildings, the streets, and the sanitary system had been neglected during the civil wars, had fallen sadly into disrepair, and now called for a constructive reorganization. By the victory over Sextus Pompey in 36 B. C., to which Agrippa had contributed so largely, the government of Octavian had recovered its prestige in Italy, but with the inevitable struggle with Antony in the offing, it was desirable to demonstrate to Italy, and particularly to Rome itself, that the government was interested in problems of reconstruction. Here was a chance for a great object-lesson as to the possibilities of Octavian's government, if, in the midst of the Dalmatian War, Octavian's greatest general could devote himself to works of peace, and in a democratic way, by assuming a minor office, although already a consular. It must have had its effect on the swing of public opinion in Octavian's favor, as against Antony, which took place towards the end of

[1] *Mem. Am. Acad. in Rome,* IX, 11-32.

this very year. In fact it was in the early weeks of the following year that Antony was proclaimed a public enemy, and war declared.

The fullest account of Agrippa's aedileship is that given by Dio,[2] who states in connection with the year 33 B. C., that "Agrippa agreed to be made aedile, and without taking anything from the public treasury he repaired all the public buildings and all the streets, cleaned out the sewers, and sailed through them underground into the Tiber." He then goes on to mention the setting up in the Circus of dolphins[3] and *ova,* to indicate the laps which had been completed; his distributions of olive oil and salt; the free baths which he furnished throughout the year to women, as well as to men; his hiring of barbers to shave the citizens free of charge on the holiday celebrations which he gave, including a celebration of the *Ludus Troiae* in which even the children of senators took part; his raining on the heads of the people in the theatre tickets which were good for money, or clothes, or other things; and his allowing the crowds to scramble for all sorts of favors which were placed in their midst. He finally comes to the sterner side of the régime as aedile, the driving out of the city of the astrologers and charlatans. It was no wonder that Horace[4] wrote at this time "scilicet ut plausus quos fert Agrippa feras tu." Strangely enough Dio in his account of Agrippa's aedileship[5] fails to mention the aqueducts which most impressed Pliny[6] and Frontinus,[7] unless they are meant to be included under *τὰ οἰκοδομήματα τὰ κοινά.* Pliny[8] in discussing the subject of the aqueducts and numerous fountains[9] compares the aedileship of Agrippa with the praetorship of Q. Marcius Rex (144 B. C.),

[2] XLIX, 43. The Greek text is cited in Appendix, p. 89.
[3] Discussed on p. 84 under Group IV.
[4] *Serm.*, II, 3, 185.
[5] He does mention the aqueducts, but in connection with the years 40 B. C. (the Julia), 34 (the Marcia), and 19 (the Virgo).
[6] *N. H.*, XXXVI, 121. Text given in Appendix, p. 91.
[7] See under Aqueducts, pp. 24 ff.
[8] *Loc. cit.*
[9] See also Strabo V, 3, 8, quoted in Appendix, p. 90.

attributing to the former, as will be shown later,[10] more than actually belonged to the year of his aedileship. He then supplements the information given by Dio in regard to the games and free baths by citing from Agrippa's own account of his aedileship the fact that *ludi* were given on fifty-nine days, "et gratuita praebita balinea CLXX."

From Dio, Pliny, Frontinus, and Strabo we have an extensive list of repairs on public buildings (unless Dio means public works in general by οἰκοδομήματα κοινὰ), streets, sewers, aqueducts, and the construction of public fountains, and in addition a lavish expenditure for games, free baths, free distributions, etc., calculated to put the plebs in a good humor. Dio states that the funds for this purpose did not come from the public treasury. From what source then did the money come? Probably, *de manubiis*. For, while Agrippa had declined a triumph for his victories in Gaul in 38/37 B. C., he was undoubtedly entitled to *manubiae*, like any other *triumphalis*, and we know that he acquired extensive estates in Sicily,[11] no doubt in connection with his naval victories in 36 B. C. As the holder of a minor public office he accomplished all that he might have achieved had he celebrated the triumphs which he had earned, and in a less ostentatious and more democratic way, financing his expenditures in the same manner as he would have done had he celebrated the triumphs.

The Sewers

As we have seen,[12] Dio states that Agrippa cleaned out the sewers (τοὺς ὑπονόμους ἐξεκάθηρε) in his aedileship, and navigated them by boat into the Tiber. Pliny, in his account of the marvels of Rome, devotes a page[13] to the sewers, commenting

[10] See p. 26.
[11] Hor., *Epistles* I, 12, 1.
[12] P. 20.
[13] Plin., *N. H.*, XXXVI, 104-108. We cite here 104, the portion which pertains to Agrippa: sed tum senes aggeris vastum spatium, substructiones Capitolii mirabantur, praeterea cloacas, opus omnium dictu maximum, subfossis montibus atque, ut paullo ante retulimus, urbe pensili subterque navigata M. Agrippae [Agrippa] in aedilitate post consulatum. The whole passage is given in Appendix, p. 91.

upon the fact that, although they carried off the normal and flood water of seven different streams, were subject to back-pressure from Tiber floods, were obliged to withstand the weight of the massive structures erected over them and the falling ruins of these same buildings as the result of fires, as well as the shock of earthquakes, they had endured for the 700 years which had elapsed since they were originally built by Tarquinius Priscus. While he states that they were "subternavigata M. Agrippae[14] in aedilitate post consulatum," he does not mention any construction, or reconstruction, by Agrippa, which would have been alien to his purpose. He may have done so in a passage, now lost, to which he refers in the words "ut paullo ante retulimus," in connection with the passage just quoted about going by boat through the sewers. Strabo was greatly impressed by the sanitary works of the Romans, in which respect they surpassed his own countrymen, and along with the aqueducts he mentions the sewers "that could wash out the filth of the city into the Tiber, which, vaulted with close-fitting stones, have in some places left room for wagons loaded with hay to pass through them."[15] Whether he connects Agrippa with the construction of sewers cannot be determined from the context since the clause *ὧν πλείστην ἐπιμέλειαν ἐποιήσατο Μάρκος Ἀγρίππας* may refer only to the aqueducts and fountains, or may include the sewers which immediately precede them in the context. We are therefore left in doubt as to the extent of Agrippa's work on the sewer system, whether it consisted merely of a "cleaning out," and inspection by boat, as Dio says, or included partial repairs and new construction. We may assume that, in connection with his extensive building operations in the Campus Martius, new sewers would be needed there, but his developments in that quarter (Groups II and III) seem to belong to the period after Actium. A large sewer, equal in size to the Cloaca Maxima, which was explored by

[14] The manuscripts vary between *Agrippae* and *Agrippa*.

[15] V, 3, 8. The whole passage is quoted in Appendix on p. 90.

Narducci in 1880 from the Piazza Mattei to the point where it entered the Tiber near the modern Ponte Garibaldi, could, from the evidence of building materials, belong to the period of Agrippa.[16]

Did Agrippa make any extensive reconstructions on the Cloaca Maxima itself? The opinion is expressed by Platner-Ashby[17] that much of its course from the Basilica Aemilia to the Tiber is assignable to the restorations of Agrippa, but with the reservation that the whole problem needs further investigation in the light of modern criteria. But if any extensive reconstruction was made by Agrippa it is difficult to understand why two almost contemporary authors, writing in the Augustan Age, should have failed to make any reference to it. Dionysius of Halicarnassus,[18] speaking of the beginning of the Cloaca by Tarquinius Priscus, mentions, on the authority of C. Aquilius, a rebuilding by certain censors (unnamed) at the enormous cost of one thousand talents. When on the subject of enormous cost of rebuilding he could hardly have ignored the work of Agrippa had it been as extensive as has been suggested by Platner-Ashby and Lugli. It is generally agreed that Book I of Livy's history was written before 25 B. C.,[19] not more than eight years after the aedileship of Agrippa. Had he been aware of the rebuilding by Agrippa of any major portion of the great sewer the language which he uses in his comparison between the past and the present in Chapter 56 is a little difficult to understand. He is there speaking of two pub-

[16] *Bull. Inst.*, 1881, p. 209; Lanciani, *R. and E.*, p. 30. Its floor, paved with *selce* like a Roman road, is 9.53 metres below the modern city. Its side walls are of massive blocks of Lapis Gabinus *(Sperone)*, with arched roof of five blocks only. The use of this stone began about 144 B. C. and it was still employed as late as the building of the walls of the Augustan Forum. (See Frank, *Rom. Build. Rep.*, p. 24.)

[17] *Top. Dict.*, p. 127. In this opinion Lugli, *Class. Monuments*, p. 353, seems to concur. Platner-Ashby, however, assigns the three concentric arches at its mouth to 100 B. C. or slightly before, in agreement with Frank, *Rom. Build. Rep.*, p. 142, n. 9.

[18] *Antiquitat.*, III, 67. He later refers in IV, 67, to the completion of the work by Tarquinius Superbus, and the construction of tunnels and arches by means of forced labor.

[19] In Book I, chap. 19, he mentions the closing of Janus in 29 B. C., but not that of 25 B. C.

lic works: (1) foros in circo faciendos, and (2) cloacamque maximam, receptaculum omnium purgamentorum urbis, sub terram agendam. He closes the sentence with these words: quibus duobus operibus vix nova haec magnificentia quicquam adaequari potuit.

In the absence of any definite statement from ancient authorities that Agrippa made any extensive restorations, the solution of this question must await further investigation, and careful weighing of the evidence furnished by building materials and construction.

THE AQUEDUCTS[20]

Agrippa's services in connection with the water-supply of Rome are the subject of comments by Strabo, Dio, and especially Frontinus, *curator aquarum* under Nerva, who in his book *de Aquis* furnishes us with most of our detailed information. From these authors we learn that his activities marked an epoch in the history of the aqueducts, not only for new construction and repairs, but also in the administration of the water-supply.

There were already in operation four aqueducts: the Appia, built in 312 B. C.; the Anio Vetus, begun in 272; the Marcia built in 144; and the Tepula in 125. For a period of nearly a century there had been no addition to the water-supply in spite of the growth of the city. Agrippa built two new aqueducts, the Julia and the Virgo, adding about one-third[21] to the existing supply, made modifications in the Tepula which improved the quality of the water, particularly as to temperature, and

[20] Two books based on the joint studies of Dr. Van Deman and Professor Ashby, as yet unpublished, should be of material aid in determining the extent of the work done by Agrippa on the Roman Aqueducts. Dr. Van Deman's manuscript, based upon a study of the building materials, is now in the hands of the Carnegie Institution for publication. Professor Ashby's was to have been published by the Oxford Press. What effect his untimely death, which all students of Roman antiquity will mourn, may have upon the ultimate publication of his book is as yet unknown to the writer. The two works on account of the thoroughness of the investigations should be the last word on the subject of the Aqueducts for some time to come.

[21] See table in Lanciani, *R. and E.*, p. 58, also sketch map *ibid.*, Fig. 19.

repaired the Appia, Anio Vetus, and the Marcia.[22] Suetonius tells that on one occasion the people complained to Augustus about the scarcity and high price of wine, and that Augustus parried the complaint with the reply that his son-in-law Agrippa had made adequate provision against thirst by bringing to the city several aqueducts.[23] Besides his work on the channels, Agrippa constructed 130 distributing reservoirs *(castella)*, 700 fountain basins *(lacus)*, 500 fountains with jets *(salientes)*, and on these works he placed 300 statues of marble and bronze, and ornamented them with 400 columns of marble.[24]

Whether Agrippa's work on the aqueducts began in 40 B. C., as Dio[25] states, or in his aedileship in 33, as we infer from Pliny[26] and Frontinus,[27] he made them his special province throughout his life and continued to be, as Frontinus[28] says, a kind of *perpetuus curator operum suorum,* a self-appointed administrator operating apparently at his own expense until his death in 12 B. C., when Augustus took over his work, using therefor certain legacies left him for the purpose by Agrippa. Agrippa maintained a regular corps of slaves *(familia)* for the care and upkeep of the aqueduct system, including the reservoirs and fountains.[29] At his death he left this *familia* by will to Augustus,[30] who converted it into a *familia publica,* which was maintained intact until the time of Frontinus (*circ.* 96 A. D.), when the force consisted of two hundred and forty men. Frontinus speaks of various details of his administration, his *commentarii,*[31] his determination of

[22] For a discussion of the chronology of these changes, see p. 26, and for the details see under the various aqueducts below.

[23] *Aug.*, 42. See also Dio LIV, 11, 7.

[24] Plin., *N. H.*, XXXVI, 121 (given in full in Appendix, p. 91). Pliny is probably mistaken in attributing all these to Agrippa's aedileship. He is certainly in error in dating the Virgo in that year. The catalogue probably came from the *Commentarii* of Agrippa, referred to in n. 31, which no doubt passed into the archives of the *curatores aquarum,* and the summary probably included all of Agrippa's work on the aqueducts. Frontinus, *de Aquis,* I, 9, also mentions the *salientes:* et singulari cura compluribus salientibus instruxit urbem. See also Strabo V, 3, 8, cited in Appendix, p. 90.

[25] XLVIII, 32, 3.

[26] *N. H.*, XXXVI, 121.

[27] *De Aquis,* I, 9.

[28] *Ibid.*, II, 98.

[29] *Ibid.*, II, 98.

[30] *Ibid.*, II, 116.

[31] *Ibid.*, II, 99.

the proportion of water which should go to public buildings, public fountains, and private individuals, and the adoption of the new *modulus,* or basis of measurement, the *quinaria.*[32]

Agrippa's practice in his self-imposed and personally financed administration of the aqueduct system no doubt became the basis for the regulations laid down for the conduct of the *curatores aquarum* in a series of decrees of the Senate passed in the year 11 B. C.,[33] when after Agrippa's death Augustus formally created the office of *curator aquarum* with Messalla Corvinus as the first incumbent. One of these contains the specific provision that the *curatores aquarum* should see to it that the number of public fountains *(publicorum salientium)* which Agrippa had constructed should not be increased or diminished.[34]

In the chronological table on page 13 it will be noted that there is some discrepancy, particularly in regard to the dating of the building of the Julia, the Virgo, and the repairs on the Marcia. In regard to the Virgo, inasmuch as Dio[35] and Frontinus[36] are in agreement in dating this aqueduct in 19 B. C., and give the consuls, we may assume that their dating is correct, and that Pliny[37] is wrong in including the Virgo among the works of Agrippa's aedileship in 33 B. C. In regard to the Julia there is more doubt. Pliny does not mention it and Frontinus and Dio are here in disagreement. Frontinus[38] states that Agrippa, serving as aedile after his consul-

[32] Frontin., *de Aquis,* I, 25; II, 99. He states, however, that there is a difference of opinion as to whether this should be ascribed to Agrippa, or to Vitruvius and the plumbers.

[33] *Ibid.,* II, 99; II, 128.

[34] *Ibid.,* II, 104. Frontinus expresses the opinion that until the building of the Claudia and Anio Novus the available supply would not admit additional diversion for fountains.

[35] LIV, 11, 7: "At his own expense he (Agrippa) brought into the city the water supply known as the Aqua Virgo, and named it the Augusta." He had already mentioned the consuls.

[36] *De Aquis,* I, 10: Idem cum iam tertium consul fuisset C. Sentio, Q. Lucretio consulibus, post annum tertium decimum quam Iuliam deduxerat, virginem quoque in agro Lucullano collectam Roman perduxit.

[37] *N. H.,* XXXVI, 121: Agrippa vero in aedilitate adiecta Virgine aqua, ceterisque conrivatis atque emendatis. He then goes on to mention the reservoirs, fountains, etc., referred to on p. 25 and in Appendix, p. 91.

[38] *De Aquis,* I, 10. For the other details see pp. 28-29.

ship, when Augustus was consul for the second time with L. Volcatius as his colleague[39] (=33 B. C.), brought this aqueduct to Rome and called it the Julia. Dio places this event in the consulship of Cn. Calvinus and Asinius Pollio (=40 B. C.). After mentioning the fact that L. Cornelius Balbus had been made *consul suffectus* at the very end of the year he goes on to say: "It was at this same time that the Aqua Julia, as it was called, was brought to Rome."[40] Are we to give greater credence to Frontinus, an expert on aqueducts, who as *curator aquarum* had studied their history, or to Dio, a historian who was not primarily interested in aqueducts, but who was gathering his information year by year from some such annalistic historian as Livy? There is this much to be said in Dio's favor that Agrippa was actually *praetor* in the year 40 B. C., and we know from Frontinus himself[41] and also from Pliny,[42] that Q. Marcius Rex in his praetorship in 144 B. C. was commissioned by the Senate to build the aqueduct which was named after him. There is therefore precedent for the building of an aqueduct by a praetor. The other three aqueducts which antedated the Julia, namely, the Appia, Anio Vetus and Tepula, were built by censors.[43] It is possible that Frontinus fell into Pliny's error in regard to the Virgo of assigning too much of Agrippa's work to his aedileship. There is also a slight difference of a year between Dio and Frontinus in the dating of the restoration of the Marcia. Dio not only mentions it among the events of 34 B. C.,[44] but specifically places it in the year before Agrippa's aedileship by introducing the account of that year and the enumeration of Agrippa's acts as aedile with the words: "the next year Agrippa agreed to be made aedile."[45] Frontinus includes the restoration of the Marcia along with the Appia and Anio Vetus in Agrippa's aedileship in 33 B. C.[46]

[39] Frontin., *de Aquis*, I, 9, has *anno post urbem conditam DCCXIX.*

[40] Dio XLVIII, 32, 3.

[41] *De Aquis*, I, 7.

[42] *N. H.*, XXXVI, 121.

[43] Frontin., *de Aquis*, I, 5; I, 6; I, 8.

[44] XLIX, 49, 2.

[45] XLIX, 43, 1.

[46] *De Aquis*, I, 9: Eodem anno (i. e., the year of Agrippa's aedileship) ductus Appiae, Anienis, Marciae paene dilapsos restituit, et singulari cura compluribus salientibus aquis instruxit urbem.

Here again it is a question as to whether more credence should be given to the historian, or to the expert on the aqueducts. There is no question about the repairs on the Appia and Anio Vetus. Dio does not mention them specifically, though he may have had them in mind in the general repairs on the *οἰκοδομήματα κοινά*.[47] Frontinus[48] places them definitely in 33 B. C., and Pliny[49] also includes them in the acts of Agrippa's aedileship.

I am inclined to think that after all the historian is more likely to be right, and that we may place the building of the Julia in 40 B. C. when Agrippa was praetor, with 33 B. C. as a possible second choice, the repairs on the Marcia in 34 B. C., the repairs on the Appia and the Anio Vetus in 33 B. C., the year of Agrippa's aedileship, and the construction of the Virgo in 19 B. C., concerning which there is no difference of opinion except in the case of Pliny.

Individual Aqueducts Built or Repaired by Agrippa

The Julia, and Additions to the Tepula

The date of these operations (40 B. C. Dio, 33 B. C. Frontinus) has been discussed in the preceding paragraphs.

The Tepula had been built in 125 B. C. by the censors Cn. Servilius Caepio and L. Cassius Longinus.[50] Its springs, which Frontinus makes a point of calling *venae* rather than *fontes*,[51] and are now called Sorgenti dell' Acqua Preziosa, were at the foot of the Alban Hills (Valle Marciana) two miles to the right of the tenth milestone of the Via Latina.[52] At that time it apparently reached the city by its own channel, of which, however, no traces have been found. As the flow was scant, and the water itself, as the name indicates, was tepid—its temperature is now 17° centigrade[53]—Agrippa undertook to great-

[47] XLIX, 43, 1.

[48] See n. 46.

[49] *N. H.*, XXXVI, 121: Agrippa vero in aedilitate adiecta Virgine aqua ceterisque conrivatis atque emendatis, etc.

[50] Frontin., *de Aquis*, I, 8.

[51] *Ibid.*, II, 68.

[52] *Ibid.*, I, 8.

[53] Lanciani, *R. and E.*, p. 51.

ly increase the flow of water and reduce its temperature by tapping a new supply, much colder and purer—the temperature is now 10° centigrade[54]—higher up the same valley at a place called Il Fontanile degli Squarciarelli di Grottaferrata, about half a mile above the Abbey. Frontinus[55] says that these new springs were two miles to the right of the twelfth milestone of the Via Latina, but, according to Ashby,[56] this distance is too far. This new supply, called the Aqua Julia, had a flow of 1206 *quinariae,* or 50,043 cubic metres in 24 hours, as compared with the original 400 *quinariae* of the Tepula. The Julia was admitted into the channel of the Tepula, about the tenth milestone of the Via Latina, and the waters of the two aqueducts were allowed to mix until they reached a common settling basin *(piscina)* between the seventh and sixth milestones.[57] Here the water, thus mixed, was divided into two conduits proportioned to the volume of the original springs, and both conduits were carried to the city on the arches of the Marcia, the Tepula immediately above the conduit of the Marcia and the Julia above the Tepula,[58] for a distance of 6,472 paces, where their remains for considerable stretches may still be seen. The three aqueducts reached Rome at the Porta Maggiore, the arches following the line of the later Aurelian wall as far as the Via Tiburtina which they crossed on a monumental archway (the existing archway was built by Augustus in 5 B. C.) and then traversed the Viminal Hill underground, emerging at the terminal castellum of the Marcia near the Colline gate.[59] Frontinus[60] states that *ad Spem Veterem* (near the modern Porta Maggiore) a part of the Julia had previously been diverted to serve the Caelian. Another branch of the Julia, not mentioned by Frontinus, but indicated upon Lanciani's *Forma Urbis Romae*, Pl. 24, was apparently diverted near the Porta

[54] *Ibid.*, p. 52.

[55] *De Aquis*, I, 9.

[56] *Top. Dict.*, p. 24.

[57] Frontin., *de Aquis*, I, 9; I, 69.

[58] *Ibid.*, I, 19.

[59] See Lanciani, *Forma Urbis Romae*, Sheets 17, 18, 24, and 32; Frontin., *de Aquis*, I, 19.

[60] I, 19.

Tiburtina and supplied the Nymphaeum, popularly called "I Trofei di Mario," at the junction of the Via Tiburtina Vetus with the Via Labicana.

Frontinus gives the following additional information in regard to the Julia and the Tepula, some of it perhaps applicable only to his own time. He gives the total length of the Julia as 15,426½ paces.[61] The length of the Tepula is not given, but it was reckoned as an independent aqueduct only from the point where the conduit emerged from the piscina of the Julia between the sixth and seventh milestones of the Via Latina.[62] He further states that the Julia served regions II, III, V, VI, VIII, X, XII,[63] and the Tepula regions IV, V, VI, VII,[64] and that the head of the Julia within the city was third[65] in height after the Anio Novus and the Claudia, and that of the Tepula fourth.[66] In his day the Tepula took 92 *quinariae* from the Marcia[67] and 190 from the Julia,[68] and its total volume was 445 *quinariae*.[69] The Julia received[70] 162 *quinariae* from the Claudia, and gave[71] 190 to the Tepula.[72]

A number of *cippi* of the Julia have come to light at different times, all belonging to later restorations by Augustus, No. 302 near the springs, 281 just below the Abbey of Grottaferrata, and 157, 156, 154, 153 near the seventh milestone of the Via Latina, before the channel emerges on the arches of the Marcia. All of these belong to a restoration which took place between 11-4 B. C.[73] Another *cippus* dating from 14 A. D. has been found above the Abbey.[74]

[61] *De Aquis*, I, 19.
[62] *Ibid.*, II, 68.
[63] *Ibid.*, II, 83.
[64] *Ibid.*, II, 82.
[65] *Ibid.*, I, 18.
[66] *Ibid.*, I, 18.
[67] *Ibid.*, II, 67.
[68] *Ibid.*, II, 68.
[69] *Ibid.*, II, 68.
[70] *Ibid.*, II, 69.
[71] *Ibid.*, II, 68.
[72] For other information concerning the Tepula not already mentioned in the notes see Frontinus, *de Aquis*, I, 4; II, 125; Lanciani, *I Commentarii di Frontino; Notit. Appendix;* Polem. Silv., 545-546; concerning the Julia: Frontinus I, 4; II, 76; II, 125; *Notit. Appendix;* Polem. Silv., *loc. cit.*
[73] *CIL*, VI, 31562—XIV, 4278; *Not. Scav.*, 1887, pp. 73, 82, 558, 559; 1914, p. 68; 1925, p. 51; *Bull. Com.*, 1886, p. 313; 1887, p. 131. See also Platner-Ashby, p. 24.
[74] *Not. Scav.*, 1893, p. 240; *CIL*, VI, 31563 c; *Eph. Epig.*, IX, 970.

The Marcia Repaired

Dio, as has been seen,[75] placed this restoration in 34 B. C.; Frontinus groups it with the repairs on the Appia and Anio, and the construction of the Julia, in Agrippa's aedileship (33 B. C.). The restoration is merely mentioned by Pliny,[76] and by Frontinus.[77] Dio gives more details (XLIX, 42): "And Agrippa restored from his own purse the water-supply named the Aqua Marcia, which was deficient because of the disrepair of the conduits, and piped it to many parts of the city." He takes this opportunity to contrast the modesty and moderation of Agrippa and of Aemilius Lepidus, who had just rebuilt the Basilica Aemilia, with the attitude of the triumph-seekers who, using the influence of Antony and of Caesar, bargained to have triumphs voted them, exacting therefor large amounts from foreign states.

This old aqueduct, constructed in 144-140 B. C. by Q. Marcius Rex, was restored again between 11 and 4 B. C. when Augustus took over the management of the aqueducts after Agrippa's death. It is to this latter restoration that the inscription on the monumental arch which carried the aqueduct over the Via Tiburtina belongs (5 B. C.),[78] as well as numerous *cippi* found along its course.[79]

Repairs on the Anio Vetus and the Appia

We have no details in regard to Agrippa's work on these aqueducts except the statement of Frontinus that during the year of Agrippa's aedileship, 33 B. C., he restored the channels of the Appia and the Anio, *paene dilapsos*.[80]

Aqua Virgo

We have already seen that Dio and Frontinus are in accord in dating this aqueduct in 19 B. C., and that Pliny's date of 33

[75] Pp. 27, 28.
[76] *N. H.*, XXXI, 41.
[77] *De Aquis*, I, 9.
[78] *CIL*, VI, 1244.
[79] See Platner-Ashby, *Top. Dict.*, p. 25.
[80] *De Aquis*, I, 9. See n. 46.

B. C. is erroneous.[81] Frontinus gives the fifth day before the Ides of June (June 9) as the day upon which the water reached the city.[82]

This aqueduct, built by Agrippa at his own expense,[83] is closely connected with his other building activities in the Campus Martius,[84] and supplied the water for the Thermae, the Stagnum, and the Euripus as well as for most of the numerous fountains mentioned by Pliny.[85] Because of its association with these haunts of pleasure-loving Romans it is frequently mentioned by the poets[86] from Ovid to Martial, and received an acclaim never accorded to Agrippa's other aqueduct, the Julia. Their praises are due partly to the park-like surroundings of the Horti Agrippae and the Campus Agrippae with their many statues and fountains, and partly to the quality of the water for bathing purposes, both in the warm baths of the Thermae, and in the open air bathing facilities offered by the Stagnum and the Euripus. The water of the Virgo was soft compared with the lime-charged water brought down from the Sabine Hills by the Marcia,[87] the Anio Vetus, and the Anio Novus, although in its drinking qualities it ranked third among all the aqueducts.

Frontinus tells us that the springs of the Virgo were located *in agro Lucullano,* at the eighth milestone from the city on the Via Collatina.[88] He ascribes the name Virgo to the fact that the springs were pointed out to the soldiers in their search for water by a maiden, and states that the incident is recorded on a painting in a little chapel located at the source. As the springs were in a swampy region the waters were first collected in a

[81] See pp. 26, 28.

[82] *De Aquis,* I, 10.

[83] Dio LIV, 11, 7.

[84] See Groups II and III.

[85] See p. 25.

[86] Ovid, *Fasti,* I, 464; *Ex Ponto,* I, 8, 38; Statius, *Silv.,* I, 5, 26; Mart., VI, 20, 9; 42, 18; VII, 32, 11; XI, 47, 6; XIV, 163. See also Sen., *Epist.,* 83, 5.

[87] Plin., *N. H.,* XXXI, 42; quantum Virgo tactu praestat, tantum praestat Marcia haustu.

[88] *De Aquis,* I, 10. Pliny, *N. H.,* XXXI, 42, says: ab octavi lapidis deverticulo duo millia passuum Praenestina via. There is really no discrepancy since the Via Collatina was two miles to the left. Pliny is wrong, however, in associating with the Virgo the Herculaneus rivus.

basin lined with *opus signinum*, a part of which still exists near the railway station of Salone. Frontinus[89] also states that the volume of water was increased by the addition of several other springs, and that the length of the aqueduct was 14,105 paces (20,697 metres), of which 12,865 paces were underground, and 1,240 above ground, 540 being carried upon substructions, and 700 paces (from the Via Capo le Case) on arches. The course of the aqueduct was toward the Porta Praenestina, but about one kilometre from this gate it swerved northward and entered the city under the Villa Medici (Horti Lucullani)[90] on the Pincian Hill. From this point it ran south along the edge of the hill, turning southwest near the Via Capo le Case, where the arches began; it then turned south along the eastern edge of the Campus Agrippae (see Fig. 4) and then westward across the Via Flaminia (at the site of the later arch of Claudius) and along the northern end of the Saepta, where its arches ended,[91] near the northwest corner of the church of S. Ignazio.

Frontinus furnishes the additional information[92] that the total volume was 2504 *quinariae*[93] (103,916 cubic metres in 24 hours), of which 200 *quinariae* were distributed outside the city, and 2304 within the city itself through regions VII, IX, and XIV,[94] to 18 *castella*. Of the 1417 *quinariae* devoted to public uses, 26 went to two *munera*,[95] 61 to twenty-five *lacus*,

[89] *De Aquis*, I, 10.

[90] *Ibid.*, I, 22: Arcus Virginis initium habent sub hortis Lucullanis, finiuntur in Campo Martio secundum frontem saeptorum.

[91] *Ibid., loc. cit.*

[92] *Ibid.*, II, 84. Some of this information may be applicable only to his own time.

[93] Frontinus, *de Aquis*, II, 70, states that this is a corrected measurement made at the second milestone, where the flow is more rapid than at the source. He states that the *Commentarii* give it as 770 *quinariae* less.

[94] Region VII was the eastern portion of the Campus Martius between the Via Flaminia and the Pincian Hill, and contained the Campus Agrippae and the Porticus Vipsania described in Group III, pp. 73-77. Region IX was the western portion of the Campus Martius, containing the major public works of Agrippa described in Group II, pp. 37-69. Region XIV was across the Tiber and we may perhaps associate the building of the Pons Agrippae (see p. 66), with the necessity of carrying the conduit across the river.

[95] Frontinus does not furnish a clue to the sense in which he is here using the word (*de Aquis*, II, 84).

and 1,330 to public buildings and public works, of which the Euripus alone received 460.

The level of the Virgo[96] was the lowest of all the aqueducts except the Appia and the Alsietina, and like them it had no settling tank in Frontinus' day,[97] though one was added later below the Pincian. For the remains within the city see Lanciani, *Forma Urbis Romae.*[98]

Cippi of Tiberius (36-37 A. D.) and Claudius (44-45 A. D.) have been found in the Villa Medici, two bearing the number I, and a third the number IIII.[99] In 46 A. D. Claudius restored the arch over a side street from the Via Lata, which had been damaged by Caligula's unfinished construction of an amphitheatre near the Saepta,[100] and in 51-52 A. D. the same emperor, to celebrate his victories in Britain, erected a triumphal arch, which also carried the Aqua Virgo across the Via Lata, opposite the northern end of the Saepta.[101] There is also a record of a restoration by Constantine.[102]

The Virgo still supplies the city with water, having been restored by Nicholas V in 1453, by Sixtus IV, and thoroughly rebuilt by Pius V in 1570. Its present terminus is the famous Trevi fountain. Now, as in the days of Agrippa,[103] it still furnishes water for many fountains, the most numerous being those built by Gregory XIII.

[96] Frontin., *de Aquis*, I, 18.

[97] *Ibid.*, I, 22.

[98] Sheets 1, 2, 9, 15, 16. See also *Bull. Com.*, 1881, pp. 61-67; 1883, pp. 6-7, 51-52; *Mitt.*, 1889, p. 269. Lanciani, *Acque*, pp. 120-130; Platner-Ashby, *Top. Dict.*, p. 28; Jordan, *Top.*, I, 1, pp. 471-472.

[99] *CIL*, VI, 1253-1254.

[100] *CIL*, VI, 1252: Ti. Claudius . . . arcus ductus aquae Virginis disturbatos per C. Caesarem a fundamentis novos fecit ac restituit. Suet., *Calig.*, 27. The arch and inscription may be seen in the courtyard of Via Nazareno, No. 14.

[101] *CIL*, VI, 920-923 = 31203-4; Suet., *Claud.*, 17; Dio IX, 19 ff; 22.

[102] *CIL*, VI, 31564, found on the site of the Exposition building on the Via Nazionale, obviously not in its original position.

[103] For Agrippa's fountains see pp. 25, 83.

GROUP II

AGRIPPA'S BUILDINGS IN THE CAMPUS MARTIUS IN REGION IX

Group II

AGRIPPA'S BUILDINGS IN THE CAMPUS MARTIUS IN REGION IX

The Saepta

The first of Agrippa's building activities in this part of the Campus Martius seems to have been the completion of one of Julius Caesar's many projects. Cicero writes to Atticus[1] in 54 B. C. of one of Caesar's grandiose plans to make of the Saepta, the traditional meeting place for the Comitia Tributa, a marble structure with a roof, and to surround it with a marble portico a mile in extent. Caesar did not live to carry out this plan, if indeed he had actually begun it, and it was carried on by Lepidus, who had twice been Caesar's master of horse during the dictatorship, probably after the second triumph of Lepidus, which was celebrated on December 31, 43 B. C., and probably from the *manubiae* connected with that triumph.[2] We may assume that Lepidus had not put the finishing touches on this colossal structure before his final break with Octavian in 36 B. C., after which he became a virtual prisoner at Circeii, since we read in Dio,[3] in connection with the events of the year 26 B. C.: "After this he (Augustus) became consul for the eighth time, together with Statilius Taurus, and Agrippa dedicated the structure called the Saepta; for, instead of undertaking to repair a road, Agrippa had adorned with stone tablets and with paintings this edifice in the Campus Martius, with porticoes all around it, for the meeting of the Comitia Tributa, and he named it the Saepta Julia in honor of Augustus." As Lepidus did not dedicate it, while he still performed his functions as triumvir up till 36 B. C., we may assume that it had not been completed structurally at the time of the break between

[1] *Att.*, IV, 16, 14.
[2] I have discussed this question in *Mem. Am. Acad. in Rome*, IX, pp. 17-18.
[3] LIII, 23.

him and Octavian, and that Agrippa did considerably more than merely decorate and dedicate the building.

The Saepta, also called the *Ovile*[4] from its resemblance to a sheepfold, was in the time of the Republic an enclosed area, inaugurated as a templum,[5] of roughly 1000 feet to a side, extending westward from the Via Flaminia and divided by barriers into aisles and sections to facilitate voting by *curiae, tribus,* or *centuriae.*[6] If Cicero's mile[7] is not a humorous exaggeration, and is to be taken seriously, it must have been Caesar's plan to erect his portico about all four sides. In that case Lepidus and Agrippa limited their structure to the side along the Via Flaminia from the foot of the Capitoline Hill to the Aqua Virgo, which Agrippa built later, leaving the area to the west as far as the Pantheon and the Baths an open space, as heretofore. The name Saepta continued in use for the whole area, as well as for the great hall and portico.[8]

The portico is partly represented on the Marble Plan,[9] and from this and the remains which have been discovered to the west of the Via Flaminia,[10] it is possible to get an idea of its ground plan. The portico was an elongated rectangle extending along the Via Flaminia on its west side from the Aqua Virgo,[11] the present Via del Caravita, to the Via di S. Marco,[12] a distance of more than 400 metres (1,400-1,500 Roman feet). It was supported by eight rows of isolated piers, both simple

[4] This word *ovile* was still occasionally used after the construction of the Saepta Julia (Liv. XXVI, 22; Lucan II, 197; Ausonius, *Grat. act.*, III, 13) though Saepta was the usual word, applied somewhat confusingly sometimes to the portico, sometimes to the area. The portico is once referred to as Porticus Saeptorum (Plin., *N. H.*, XVI, 201), and once in the third century as Saepta Agrippiana (*Vit. Alexand.*, 26).

[5] Cic., *Pro Rab.*, 11.

[6] Platner-Ashby, *Top. Dict.*, p. 373.

[7] *Att.*, IV, 16, 14.

[8] See n. 4.

[9] Jordan, *FUR*, 35-36.

[10] Huelsen-Jordan, *Top.*, I[3], p. 460; *Bull. Com.*, 1893, pp. 125-128; *Not. Scav.*, 1911, p. 36. Platner-Ashby, *Top. Dict.*, p. 461.

[11] See p. 33, n. 94, also Fig. 4.

[12] Lanciani, *Ruins and Excavations*, p. 472, thought it ended at a cross street found in 1875 under the side door of the Church of S. Marco, but the evidence of the antiquity of the street is not conclusive, and besides masonry probably belonging to the porticus has been found under the Palazzetto di Venezia (Platner-Ashby, p. 461).

and compound, of rusticated travertine, upon which rest the springs of the cross-vaulting,[13] as may be seen from a drawing by Piranesi.[14] Four inner piers of the fourth and fifth rows under the Palazzo Doria were measured by Huelsen who found that they were 1.70 metres square, 4 metres apart in the north-south direction, and 6.20 metres on the east-west line. The width of the portico from east to west was 60 metres (= 200 Roman feet). Remains of brick pilasters of the time of Hadrian under the Banco di Roma point to a restoration by that emperor.

Was this structure, which conforms to the Marble Plan of the beginning of the third century, the work of Lepidus and Agrippa? We know that it was damaged in the fire of Titus in 80 B. C., and probably restored by Domitian, since it was one of the haunts of Martial.[15] It was restored, as we have seen, under Hadrian.[16] The travertine pilasters are at any rate more characteristic of the Augustan Age than of the later periods. With the diminishing importance of its original function, the holding of elections, some changes in its inner arrangement may well have been made.

It was used for other purposes even in the time of Augustus. The Senate met here on May 23 in connection with the Ludi Saeculares of 17 B. C.;[17] part of the games with which Augustus celebrated the fifth anniversary of the death of Agrippa were held in the Saepta (7 B. C.),[18] as were also some of the games (gladiatorial combats) in celebration of the dedication of the Forum Augusti (2 B. C.).[19] In it, in 9 A. D., Augustus received Tiberius on his victorious return from his Illyrian Campaign, and Tiberius addressed the people from a platform erected in it.[20] Caligula gave *munera gladiatoria* in the

[13] Rivoira, *Roman Architecture*, pp. 93-95.
[14] *Campo Marzio*, Pl. XXV; *Antichita di Roma*, IV, p. 47.
[15] See n. 28.
[16] This restoration, mentioned in *Vit. Hadr.*, 19, is confirmed by brick-stamps.
[17] *Act. Lud. Saec.*, *CIL*, VI, 32323, line 50.
[18] Dio LV, 8, 5.
[19] Dio LV, 10, 17; Suet., *Aug.*, 43.
[20] Suet., *Tib.*, 17; Dio LVI, 1.

Saepta,[21] also Claudius,[22] and Nero gave gymnastic contests there.[23] These various performances, as well as the naval exhibition of Caligula,[24] for which he excavated an artificial lake, were said by Suetonius to have been held *in Saeptis,* and must have been given in the open area to the west of the portico, referred to by Statius[25] as *patula Saepta,* while the arcades of the portico, and its roof, must have been used for the seating of the spectators.

Seneca speaks of the crowds which in his day frequented it;[26] Pliny speaks of two works of art which it contained, both by unknown artists, one a group of Olympus and Pan, the other of Chíron and Achilles;[27] Martial[28] speaks of it as a favorite lounging-place and a bazaar where all sorts of wares were sold: citrus furniture, works of ivory, bronzes, murrhine vases, silver cups, gems, pearls, and even slaves.

In the later empire it is mentioned in the third century as *Saepta Agrippiana,*[29] and the name Saepta occurs on the bronze collar of a slave belonging to post-Constantinian times.[30] Strangely enough, there is no reference to it in the *Notitia* and *Curiosum* or in the literature of the Middle Ages.

The Diribitorium

Functionally, if not actually, connected with the Saepta is another structure ascribed to Agrippa—the Diribitorium—which also had to do originally with the elections, and was apparently the place where the 900 election judges in the time of Augustus kept the voting urns and counted the votes.[31]

Dio gives us an account of it among the events of the year 7 B. C.:[32] "The Campus Agrippae and the Diribitorium were

[21] Suet., *Calig.*, 18.
[22] Suet., *Claud.*, 21.
[23] Suet., *Nero*, 12.
[24] Dio LIX, 10, 5.
[25] *Silv.*, IV, 5, 2.
[26] *De Ira*, II, 81.
[27] *N. H.*, XXXVI, 29. Martial also mentions the second of these groups (II, 14, 6).
[28] II, 14, 5; 57, 2; IX, 59, 1; X, 80, 4.
[29] *Vit. Alexand.*, 26.
[30] *CIL*, XV, 7195: tene me quia fugio et revocà me in saeptis.
[31] Plin., *N. H.*, XXXIII, 31.
[32] Dio LV, 8, 3-4 (for Greek text see Appendix, p. 90).

made public property by Augustus himself. The Diribitorium was the largest building under a single roof ever constructed; indeed, now that the whole covering has been destroyed,[33] the edifice is wide open to the sky (ἀχανής), since it could not be put together again. Agrippa had left it in process of construction, and it was completed at this time.'' Pliny speaks of this marvelous roof,[34] and of one of the beams left over from its construction which lay in the long portico of the Saepta, obviously as a museum exhibit. This beam was of larch, 100 feet long and a foot and a half thick.[35]

If this building, of such proportions that it was used as an indoor theatre by Caligula when the sun was excessively hot,[36] was a separate structure, where could it have stood, and why was it allowed to remain roofless for the century and a third which intervened between the fire of Titus and the time when Dio wrote his history, in a location which was rapidly becoming more and more valuable with the extension of the city over the Campus Martius; also, why have no traces of it been found in the vicinity of the Saepta with which it was functionally connected? Huelsen[37] answers this question by assuming that it was constructed *on top of* the Saepta Julia, whose pillars seemed to him too sturdy for the support of a mere portico, but rather to have been built to carry a superstructure. That its elevation was high we may assume from a statement of Suetonius that Claudius, during a stubborn fire in the quarter known as the *Aemiliana,* remained in the Diribitorium for two nights, presumably watching the efforts to control it.[38]

Huelsen's theory has in its favor only two considerations:

[33] In the fire which occurred in 80 A. D. (Dio LXVI, 24).

[34] *N. H.*, XXXVI, 102: non et tectum Diribitori ab Agrippa facti (inter magna opera dicamus)?

[35] Plin., *N. H.*, XVI, 201: fuit memoria nostra et in porticibus Saeptorum trabes e larice a M. Agrippa relicta, aeque miraculi causa, quae Diribitorio superfuerat xx pedibus brevior (than the beam of 120 feet which he had described in the previous sentence) sesquipedali crassitudine.

[36] Dio LIX, 7.

[37] *Bull. Com.*, 1893, p. 137. See also Jordan-Huelsen, *Top.*, I^3, p. 562; Platner-Ashby, *Top. Dict.*, p. 151.

[38] *Claud.*, 18. (See Appendix, p. 92.)

(1) the fact that functionally the Diribitorium was connected with the counting of the votes in the elections which were held in the Saepta; and (2) the huge timber which lay in the long portico of the Saepta, which may, after all, have been placed there simply as an exhibit. There are four rather strong arguments against it: (1) Dio, in LV, 8, 3-4 (see n. 32) seems to be speaking of the Diribitorium as a separate building, without any mention of the Saepta; (2) the natural query as to why it was not completed until twenty years after the dedication of the Saepta, if it was an integral part of that structure; (3) Dio, in his records of the buildings of the Campus Martius, which were destroyed by the fire of Titus, again not only mentions it as a separate building, but does not list it with the Saepta, where one would expect to find it, but between the Pantheon and the Theatre of Balbus,[39] a position which Huelsen has had to explain away on the assumption that the unusual word *Diribitorion* had been omitted by a scribe and had been reintroduced in the wrong place;[40] (4) its proximity to the district known as the Aemiliana. In regard to this last, Huelsen himself admits that if *CIL*, XV, 7150, was correctly copied (it exists only in a Sixteenth Century copy) this quarter was on the Tiber north of the Theatre of Balbus near the Palazzo Farnese.[41] Claudius could have had a better and also a closer view of a fire raging in this district from the Capitol than from the upper story of the Saepta.

The evidence would seem to point to a location somewhere within a triangle whose three points would be the Pantheon, the Theatre of Balbus, and the Aemiliana, which, as we have seen, was located somewhere near the modern Palazzo Farnese. Are there any ruins in this area, of sufficient magnitude to have served as the foundations for the Diribitorium, which have not been positively identified as belonging to other known

[39] LXVI, 24, cited in Appendix, p. 90. [40] *Bull. Com.*, 1893, p. 138, n. 2.

[41] *Top.*, I³, 490. That it was outside the city limits is shown by Varro, *De R. R.*, III, 2, 6: Nihilo magis ideo est villa, quam eorum aedificia qui habitant extra portam Flumentanam aut in Aemilianis.

structures? A glance at Lanciani's *Forma Urbis Romae,* Pl. 21, suggests one such possibility, namely, the structure now represented by the two travertine pilasters with engaged columns which stand in the Via dei Calderari 23, identified tentatively by Lanciani as belonging to the Crypta Balbi and by Huelsen as belonging to the Porticus Minucia. If Lanciani's ground plan is correct, this structure was of a size commensurate with the huge roof mentioned by Dio and by Pliny. Lundström,[42] in fact, in his recent work has sought to identify this structure with the Diribitorium. Its dimensions, 148.5 by 45.5 metres, could well correspond with the great hall for the nine hundred *diribitores,* requiring roof beams one hundred feet long, and this identification at first sight seems attractive. But Boethius in his exhaustive review of Lundström's work in *Athenaeum,* 1932,[43] points out (pp. 117-121) that, while the pilasters may be Augustan, the *opus concretum* and the brick work seem to belong to the time of Domitian, and that the structure in Domitian's time took the form of a portico of two stories (as is shown in a drawing of Sangallo the elder)[44] which would not have been hard to roof, while Dio states that the Diribitorium stood open to the sky in his day because of the difficulty of replacing its enormous roof. Consequently, unless the second period of construction was later than Dio, this building cannot have been the Diribitorium. If Boethius is right,[45] this attractive possibility suggested by Lundström will have to be abandoned, and the location of the Diribitorium relegated to the area west of a line drawn from the Pantheon to the Theatre of Balbus, much of which is still a *terra incognita* from the archaeological and the topographical point of view.

[42] Lundström, *Undersökningar i Roms topografi* (*Svenskt Arkiv för humanistika avhandligar* II) Goteburg, 1929.

[43] See also Boethius and Nettelbladt, *Eranos,* 1931, pp. 83-97, where the structure is identified as Crypta Balbi, and Ashby's review of Lundström's article, *Gnomon,* 1932, p. 485, which is in general accord with the views of Boethius.

[44] *Cod. Barberin.,* fol. 1, reproduced in Lanciani, *R. and E.,* p. 495, fig. 194.

[45] Boethius, *loc. cit.,* however, quotes Van Deman as expressing the verbal opinion, based upon construction and materials, that the second period may have been later than the time of Domitian.

Porticus Argonautarum and Basilica Neptuni

Dio, in narrating the events of the year 25 B. C., mentions three buildings which Agrippa completed in that year in his program of beautifying the city at his own expense. First in the list[46] is the building which Dio calls *τὴν στοὰν τοῦ Ποσειδῶνος*, erected by Agrippa in honor of his naval victories, and adorned with a painting representing the Argonauts.[47] Although Agrippa consistently refused to celebrate a triumph,[48] reserving this honor for Augustus alone, it was only fitting that he, as the actual victor both in the campaign against Sextus Pompey in 36 B. C., and again in the campaign of 31 B. C., should have accorded to him the privilege, assumed by all the *triumphales* mentioned in our previous paper,[49] of erecting a building to commemorate his naval victories. A scene or a series of scenes from the voyage of the Argonauts would be more in keeping with the modesty of his character than actual scenes from his own victories, as indirectly suggesting rather than frankly proclaiming his own services. Dio does not inform us whether the victories referred to are those of the Actian campaign exclusively, or whether the naval victories of 36 B. C. were also included in the commemoration.

This structure of Agrippa presents certain problems both in regard to its location, and whether the Porticus Argonautarum and the Basilica Neptuni, mentioned in the regionary catalogues of Region IX, are one and the same building or two separate ones. Two elements enter into Dio's account of Agrippa's building: (1) its connection with Neptune, and (2) with the painting of the Argonauts. As Dio was writing at the beginning of the third century, though no doubt using older annalistic sources, it will be well to follow through the references in the literature in chronological order. Three passages in

[46] The other two are the Laconicum Sudatorium and the Pantheon.
[47] Dio LIII, 27. The Greek text is given in the Appendix, p. 89.
[48] See p. 10.
[49] *Mem. Am. Acad. in Rome*, IX, 1931, pp. 9-44.

Martial[50] refer to the structure, though not specifically by name, as a favorite haunt and lounging-place in his day. In the first of these "An spatia carpit lentus Argonautarum" it is clear that he is referring to a promenade of some length, named from the Argonauts and presumably the Porticus Argonautarum and, in the second, the mention of Aesonides (i. e., Jason) in the same context as the Saepta with its painting of Phillyrides (i. e., Chiron) indicates close proximity to that structure. Juvenal in the sixth Satire (VI, 153-154) mentions "Mercator Iason" in a passage which would be obscure enough were it not illuminated by a scholion, to which we shall refer later,[51] which states that the reference is to a painting *in porticu Agrippiana* at Rome. In his account of the buildings damaged by the fire of Titus,[52] Dio again mentions *τὸ Ποσειδώνιον*. It is preceded in the list by the Saepta, and immediately followed by the Baths of Agrippa and the Pantheon. This serves to indicate its location. The life of Hadrian, in the *Historia Augusta,* states that that emperor restored the Pantheon, the Saepta, and the Basilica Neptuni.[53] The grouping is about the same as in the passage in Dio.

From these passages we have the following names: *ἡ στοὰ τοῦ Ποσειδῶνος* and *τὸ Ποσειδώνιον* of Dio, Basilica Neptuni, Porticus Agrippiana, and in the passage in Martial a porticus which went by the name of the Argonauts. Thus far we might assume that all these references referred to one building. When we come to the *Notitia* and the *Curiosum*[54] we find that both have in Region IX Porticus Argonautarum but that the *Curiosum* has in addition Basilica Neptuni, while the *Notitia,* which omits the Basilica Neptuni, has included a building called the Hadrianeum omitted in the *Curiosum.* In the Appendix, each of these regionaries lists under the head of basilicas a Basilica

[50] Mart., II, 14, 6; III, 20, 11; XI, 1, 2.
[51] P. 46.
[52] LXVI, 24, 2. For the Greek text see Appendix, p. 90.
[53] *Vit. Hadr.*, 19, cited in Appendix, p. 92.
[54] Cited in Appendix, p. 93.

of Neptune (*"Neptuni"* in the *Notitia*, *"Neptunia"* in the *Curiosum*).[55] We thus have raised the problem of two buildings, the *Porticus Argonautarum*, and a *Basilica Neptuni*.

Perhaps the most important passage in connection with this problem is the scholion on Juvenal VI, 153-154:

> Mense quidem brumae, quo iam mercator Iason
> Clausus, et armatis obstat casa candida nautis

which explains the passage as follows:[56] that at the time of the Saturnalia the vendors of little images, which were used for presents, had been accustomed, in Juvenal's time, to set up their *casas de linteo* in the Porticus Agrippiana at Rome, on which was painted the story of the Argonauts, and that at such times these canvas booths obstructed the view of the painting.

On the basis of this passage Huelsen,[57] following the studies of Lucas,[58] concludes that the Ποσειδώνιον, or Basilica Neptuni, was not identical with the Porticus Argonautarum, but that they were closely connected, and that the scholion on the passage in Juvenal can best be explained on the assumption that the paintings of the Argonauts were on an outer wall of the Basilica Neptuni, which adjoined one side of the portico. The booths of the vendors in the portico, at the time of the Saturnalia, thus temporarily shut off the view of the paintings of Jason and the Argonauts on the outer wall of the basilica. He believes that Lucas has successfully shown that the later Hadrianeum, of which eleven columns are still standing in the Piazza di Pietra, where they flank the north side of the

[55] *Curiosum:* Basilicae x. Iulia. Ulpia. Pauli. Bestilia. Neptunia. Matidies. Marcianes. Vascolaria. Floscolaria. Constantiniana.

Notitia: Basilicae x. Iulia. Ulpia. Pauli. Vestidia. Neptuni. Matidies. Martianes. Bascellaria. Floscellaria. Constanti*ni*ana.

[56] "Casa candida" illud significat, quod Romae in porticu thermarum Traianarum tempore Saturnalium sigillaria sunt. Tunc mercatores casas de linteo faciunt, quibus picturam obstruunt. Ideo autem dicit "mercator Iason," quoniam antea in porticu Agrippiana Roma sigillaria proponebantur, in qua porticu historia Argonautarum depicta est, ut casae cum fierent, picturae obstabant.

[57] *Jahreshefte des Oesterreichischen Arch. Instituts*, 1912, p. 132 ff.

[58] *Zur Geschichte der Neptunsbasilica in Rom* (Berlin, 1904).

building of the Bourse, was built within the area surrounded by the Porticus Argonautarum. If the Porticus Argonautarum is to be identified with the portico surrounding the Hadrianeum, it enclosed a rectangular area 108 metres long from east to west, and 98 metres wide.[59] Remains of it have been found on the north and west sides, and its whole circuit may therefore be plotted. Its southeast corner came very close to the northwest corner of the Saepta, and this location fits in very well with one of the passages in Martial, already referred to.[60] If Huelsen is correct in his conclusion that one of the outer walls of the basilica bordered one of the sides of the portico, the question remains as to which side the basilica adjoined. Huelsen concludes that it could have been located only on the west side, partly because of the order of the buildings listed in the *Notitia* and *Curiosum*,[61] and partly because there alone could room be found for a large building, although no certain remains of such a building have been found there.[62] If the basilica was 100 feet broad, its west side would have extended as far as the apse of S. Maria in Aquiro.

The words *Neptuni* and Ποσειδώνιον might suggest the presence in the neighborhood of a temple or shrine of Neptune, but of this there is no other evidence. The name, like that of the porticus, may have been derived from some statue or painting incidental to the commemoration of Agrippa's naval victories.

The Baths (τὸ πυρατήριον τὸ Λακωνικὸν and the Thermae)

What appears to have been the first unit of a larger bathing establishment is mentioned by Dio among the events of 25 B. C. He speaks of three buildings completed by Agrippa in that year, the Stoa of Poseidon, *τὸ πυρατήριον τὸ Λακωνικὸν*, and the

[59] Lanciani, *Ruins and Excavations*, p. 487.
[60] II, 14, 6. See p. 45.
[61] Huelsen, *op. cit.*, (see n. 57) p. 134.
[62] Huelsen, *op. cit.*, p. 135, speaks of some remains found in 1779 when an extension of the Palazzo Serlupi was being made in the direction of the Vicolo delle Paste, but they seem to belong to very late times if not to a Christian Church.

Pantheon.[63] In the case of the second he goes on to explain that Agrippa "gave the name Laconian to the gymnasium because the Lacedaemonians had a greater reputation at that time than any one else for stripping and exercising after anointing themselves with oil." He would have performed a greater service had he explained πυρατήριον, but we may gather from Vitruvius[64] that it meant a *sudatorium,* or sweating room, with or without a water basin. The structure must have been of considerable proportions to be mentioned along with the Basilica Neptuni and the Pantheon, but until the completion of the Aqua Virgo in 19 B. C. it could not have served as the fully equipped βαλανεῖον which Agrippa left in his will to the Roman people in 12 B. C., along with his gardens,[65] with provision for their future upkeep. We may therefore assume that the original plan must have had considerable additions made to it about 19 B. C. when Agrippa completed the Aqua Virgo. Some irregularities in the later ground plan serve to corroborate this assumption.[66] The bathing establishment, thus enlarged, which Agrippa left to the Roman people in his will, is henceforth usually referred to as *Thermae Agrippae,*[67] even after later restorations, or simply *thermae.* Pliny mentions works of art with which Agrippa decorated it: small paintings in the hottest portion of the bath,[68] painted tiles in the curved vaults *(camaras)* of the hot rooms,[69] and the Apoxyomenus of Lysippus[70] which Agrippa placed in front of the baths. This

[63] Dio LIII, 27, 1, Greek text given in Appendix, p. 89.

[64] V, 10: Laconicum sudationesque sunt coniungendae tepidario; eaeque quam latae fuerint, tantam altitudinem habeant ad imam curuaturam hemisphaerii. Cf. also V, 11, 2.

[65] Dio LIV, 29, 4, text given in Appendix, p. 89. For the Gardens see p. 53.

[66] See Fig. 1.

[67] But *lavacrum* Agrippae in *Vit. Hadr.,* 19, and *balnea* . . . quae Agrippa dedit in Sidon. Apoll., *Carm.,* 23, 496.

[68] *N. H.,* XXXV, 26: (Agrippa) in thermarum quoque calidissimo parte marmoribus incluserat parvas tabellas, paullo ante, cum reficerentur, sublatas.

[69] *N. H.,* XXXVI, 189: Agrippa certe in thermis, quas Romae fecit, figlinum opus encausto pinxit in calidis, reliqua albario adornavit, non dubie vitreas facturus camaras, si prius inventum id fuisset.

[70] *N. H.,* XXXIV, 62: inter quae distrigentem se, quem M. Agrippa ante thermas suas dicavit, mire gratum Tiberio principi. Non quivit temperare se in eo . . . transtulitque in cubiculo alio signo substituto . . .

statue was such a favorite with the people that when Tiberius removed it to his own chamber and substituted another they raised such a clamor in the theatre that the emperor was induced to replace it. Strabo[71] mentions the fallen lion of Lysippus which Agrippa brought from Lampsacus and placed in his Gardens between the Stagnum and the Euripus. This artificial lake, and the ornamental canal, to be described later,[72] supplied with water from the Aqua Virgo, were really a part of the bathing facilities of the Thermae, and took the place of the usual *frigidarium* and the *piscina,* for open air swimming, so commonly provided in the arrangements of the later Thermae.[73]

The Thermae were burned in the great fire of Titus[74] (80 A. D.) along with most of Agrippa's buildings in Region IX. They must have been at once restored by Titus or Domitian, since Martial in Book III[75] (87-88 B. C.) indicates that they were much frequented. Hadrian, who rebuilt the Pantheon, also restored the Thermae.[76] Huelsen believes that he also connected them with the Pantheon by a series of halls, remains of which still exist adjoining the Pantheon on the south.[77] Rivoira finds evidence that the great circular hall of the Baths, known as the Arco della Ciambella, with the earliest known example of meridian ribs in its dome, belonged to a reconstruction not earlier than the time of Alexander Severus.[78] A res-

[71] XIII, 1, 9, p. 590, given in Appendix, p. 90.

[72] See p. 53.

[73] Huelsen, *Thermen des Agrippa,* p. 33.

[74] Dio LXVI, 24, given in Appendix, p. 90.

[75] 20, 15; 36, 6.

[76] *Vit. Hadr.,* 19: Romae instauravit Pantheum, saepta . . . lavacrum Agrippae. See also *CIL,* VI, 9727 = 33815a.

[77] Huelsen, *(loc. cit.)* thinks that this portion (cut through by the Via della Palombella) with its beautiful marble decorations may have served as an assembly room and social hall. Lanciani wrongly calls it Laconicum, as there are no traces of heating arrangements. That there was any connection between the baths and the large hall adjoining the Pantheon has recently been called in question by von Gerkan, see p. 53, n. 90. The long corridor-like hall with an apse at each end, which appears in Huelsen's plan (fig. 2), should therefore be regarded as problematical.

[78] *Roman Architecture (Oxf., 1925),* pp. 126-7; 175-6. The hall is now only partially preserved. The existing portion may be seen in the Via dell' Arco della Ciambella.

toration by Constantius and Constans in 354-5 A. D. is recorded on an inscription found near S. Maria di Monterone not far from the west side of the baths, and probably refers to them.[79] The baths are mentioned in the *Notitia* in Region IX, by Sidonius Apollinaris,[80] and in the sixth century by Gregory the Great.[81] In the Middle Ages the whole district was known as the Calcararium,[82] showing that the marbles of the Thermae had become a prey to the lime-burner, though considerable sections of the brick and concrete parts of the structure were still standing in the fifteenth and sixteenth centuries and were sketched by numerous artists and architects.

By a careful comparison of a fragment[83] of the Marble Plan of Severus, inscribed with the words [Th]ermae [Agrip]pae, and the plans and drawings[84] of these sixteenth century architects, with the existing ruins and the meager results of excavations, Huelsen[85] has succeeded in working out a satisfactory ground plan[86] for the central and southern portion of the Baths included in the fragment of the Marble Plan. His plan for this portion is reproduced in Figure 1, and his more extended plan for the whole area including the Pantheon in Figure 2. The letters refer to Figure 1. The huge circular hall (unnumbered), the famous Arco della Ciambella, 25 metres in diameter, was probably not one of the bathing rooms, but a social centre of the baths. Huelsen identifies A as a caldarium, B and G as tepidaria, C as the Laconicum referred to by Dio, D

[79] *CIL*, VI, 1165: Termas vetustate labefactas. An earlier restoration by Commodus is possible in view of the fact that in the *Anon. Einsied.* the baths are mentioned as Thermae Commodianae: 1, 4; 2, 4; 4, 8; 8, 6. He may have read an inscription recording a restoration by that emperor.

[80] *Carm.*, 23, 496.

[81] Greg. Magn., *Reg.*, VI, 42; IX, 137: monasterium iuxta thermas Agrippianas.

[82] Jordan, *Top.*, II, p. 439, and Appendix, p. xvii; Lanciani, *Storia degli Scavi*, I, 24 f.; Huelsen, *Thermen des Agrippa*, p. 10 sq.

[83] Found in the Forum in 1900 in front of the Basilica Julia. For the literature see *Not. Scav.*, 1900, 633-4; *Bull. Com.* 1901, 3-19; Lanciani, *Storia degli Scavi*, II, 209; *Mitt.*, 1905, p. 75; Huelsen, *Thermen des Agrippa*, p. 16 ff.

[84] Particularly a drawing of Baldassare Peruzzi (Uffizi 456), another by Palladio in the Devonshire Collection (port. ix, fol. 14), and a roughly sketched plan of the Ciambella by Salvestro Peruzzi (Uffizi 642).

[85] *Thermen des Agrippa* (Rome, 1910), p. 12 ff.

[86] *Op. cit.*, Pls. III and IV.

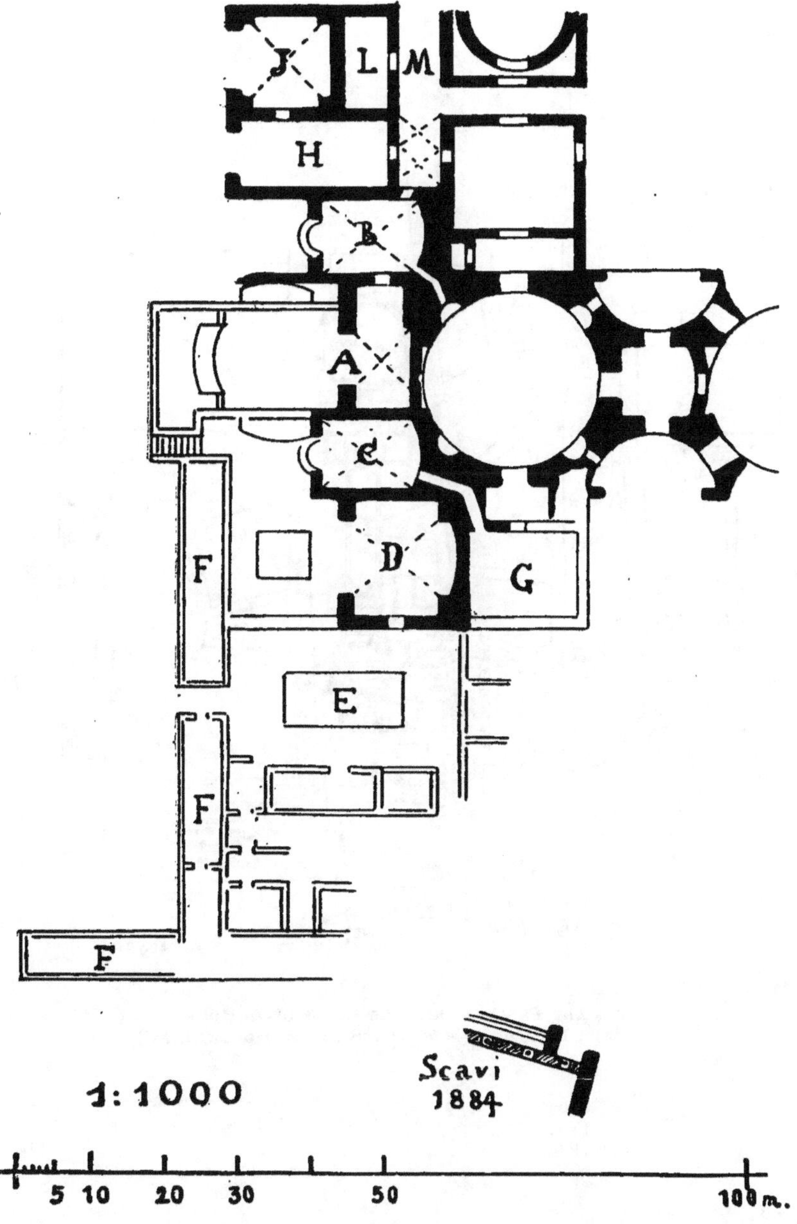

Fig. 1
Huelsen's plan of the Baths of Agrippa from *Die Thermen des Agrippa*, Pl. III

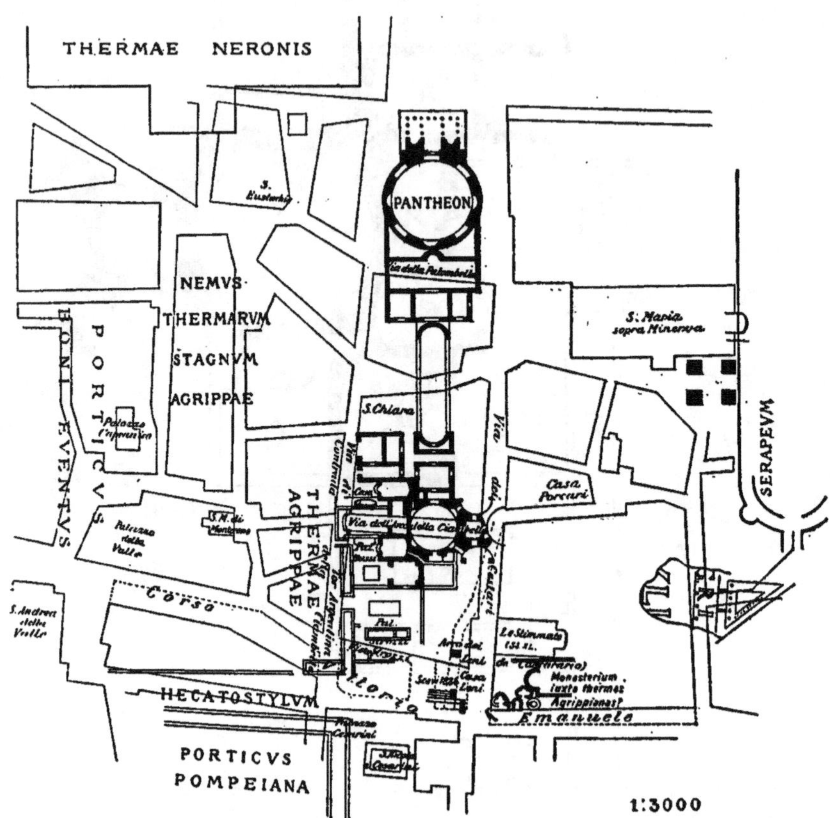

Fig. 2
The Pantheon and the Baths of Agrippa
(From Huelsen, *Die Thermen des Agrippa*, Pl. IV)

and E possibly as frigidaria, served by the corridor F. H, J, and L seem to correspond to the sphaeristeria in the small baths in Hadrian's villa. The plan bears a striking resemblance to the larger thermae at Treves.[87]

It will be noted in Figure 2 that the west front of the baths parallels, at a distance of about 50 metres, a line drawn through the centre of the Pantheon and of the Arco della Ciambella, although the axes of the two do not quite coincide. Whether the baths were developed symmetrically on the east side of this line, across the Via dei Cestari, cannot be determined. Huelsen believes that the plan of the central portion of the baths was essentially that of Agrippa and was followed by the various restorers.[88] The halls adjoining the Pantheon, however, belong to the restoration of that structure by Hadrian.[89] It will be noted that Huelsen's plan (Fig. 2) connects the baths with these halls and the Pantheon by a long corridor with an apse at each end. The existence of this corridor has recently been called in question by von Gerkan,[90] who points out that on Lanciani's large map (Pl. 21), there is indicated in the Via Sta. Chiara, slightly to the west of the supposed connecting hall, a canal or gutter which must have lined a street running eastward to the Tetrapylon, which formed the monumental entrance to the Serapeum, and that this street must have separated the Thermae from the Pantheon group.[91]

The Horti, the Stagnum, and the Euripus

Besides the facilities for warm baths furnished by the Laconicum and the Thermae, Agrippa also provided ample opportunity for open air bathing and swimming by creating an artificial lake, the Stagnum,[92] and an ornamental canal, the

[87] Anderson, Spiers, Ashby, *The Architecture of Ancient Rome* (London, 1927), p. 100, n. 1. [88] *Op. cit.*, p. 43, n. 14.

[89] See Platner-Ashby, *Top. Dict.*, p. 519, for the extensive literature on the subject.

[90] *Gnomon*, 1929, p. 277.

[91] See under Pantheon, p. 61.

[92] Ovid, *Ex Ponto*, I, 8, 38: Gramine nunc Campi pulchros spectantis in hortos stagnaque et Euripi, Virgineusque liquor. Strabo XIII, 1, 19 (see Appendix p. 90); Tac., *Ann.*, XV, 37, cited in n. 96.

Euripus,[93] for which the water was supplied by the Aqua Virgo,[94] completed in 19 B. C. The Stagnum appears to have occupied the space between the Via di Monterone and the Via dei Sediari.[95] It has usually been supposed that this is the Stagnum Agrippae referred to by Tacitus, *Ann.*, XV, 37, in which case it was large enough to enable Tigellinus, the favorite of Nero, to build a pleasure barge upon it on which he served banquets to his guests. The barge was towed about on its waters by other boats while the grove and the buildings which fringed the lake echoed with the sounds of their revelry.[96] If this is so, we should have to assume a lake of considerable proportions. It is possible, however, as has been suggested to me by Dr. Boethius, that Tacitus was there referring to Lake Avernus and the artificial harbor where Agrippa assembled his fleet for the campaign of 36 B. C. against Sextus Pompey. The Euripus, which seems to have supplied the Stagnum with water and also to have served as its outlet to the Tiber, received one-sixth of the total flow of the Aqua Virgo, and this quantity of water, amounting to 19,090 cubic metres per day,[97] insured a constant change of water in the canal itself and in the Stagnum. Seneca[98] speaks of his habit, as a younger man, of beginning the new year with a plunge in the icy waters of the Euripus, and we also have a number of references in other writers to swimming either in the lake, or in the canal.[99] The Euripus

[93] Ovid, *loc. cit.;* Sen., *Epist.*, 83, 5, see n. 98; Frontin., *de Aquis,* II, 84; Strabo XIII, 1, 19 (p. 590), see n. 92.

[94] Frontin., *loc. cit.* See previous note. [95] Huelsen, *Top.*, I³, p. 580.

[96] Tac., *Ann.*, XV, 37: igitur in Stagno Agrippae fabricatus est ratem, cui superpositum convivium navium aliarum tractu moveretur . . . crepidinibus Stagni lupanaria adstabant inlustribus feminis completa . . . iam gestus motusque obsceni; et postquam tenebrae incedebant, quantum iuxta nemoris et circumiecta tecta consonare cantu et luminibus clarescere. [97] See p. 33, n. 95.

[98] *Epist.*, 83, 5: ille tantus psychrolutes, qui Kalendis Januariis Euripum salutabam, qui anno novo quemadmodum legere, scribere, dicere aliquid, sic auspicabar in Virginem desilire, etc.

[99] No certain traces of the Euripus of Agrippa have been found. In 1930, however, in running trenches for the foundations for a new building of the Società Romana dei Beni Immobili in the angle between the Corso Vittorio Emanuele, il Lungotevere degli Altoviti, and the Via Paola, the excavators came on the remains of a Euripus, at a point where it was crossed by an ornamental footbridge of Luna marble. This bridge, 3.20 m. wide, was approached by means of three steps at each end. Romanelli in his report in *Not. Scav.*, 1931, pp. 313-317, assigns this bridge

and the Stagnum were surrounded by a park,[100] the Horti Agrippae, which extended westward towards the river,[101] and probably also some little distance eastward from the Thermae. The park must have contained a goodly number of the 300 statues with which Pliny[102] says Agrippa adorned this quarter of the city. We know of at least one, the fallen lion of Lysippus mentioned by Strabo,[103] who says that Agrippa brought it from Lampsacus and set it up in the grove (ἄλσει) between the Stagnum (λίμνης) and the Euripus. There must have been many others. The Laconicum, the Thermae, the lake, the canal, and the gardens constituted an *ensemble* which became a favorite haunt for the pleasure-loving classes. They are frequently mentioned by the poets,[104] and particularly by Martial, who lived at a time when the Baths of Nero and of Titus had already been built.

The Pantheon

Dio, in narrating the events of B. C. 25, after mentioning the completion of the Basilica of Neptune and the Laconicum

to the early empire. The canal itself is not so easily datable, although naturally it is either contemporaneous with or antedates the bridge. The canal was 3.35 m. wide and 1.73 m. deep, and the bottom of its channel had a semicircular section. The remains of what was apparently the same canal were found by Arieti in the Via del Pavone (*Bull. Com.*, 1886, p. 282) and later by Lanciani near the Piazza Sforza Cesarini (*Mon. Lincei*, I, Col. 542 ff., Pl. III). The three traces of the canal are in line, and the general direction parallels the northeast side of the present Corso Vittorio Emanuele. The section found by Lanciani, (see *R. and E.*, Fig. 174) fringes the Ara Ditis, and its orientation clearly bears some relation to that monument. This section is probably contemporaneous with a rebuilding of the Ara, either for the Secular Games of 17 B. C. or of 88 A. D. Now the Aqua Virgo, with which the Euripus was connected, was built in 19 B. C., and, in the celebration of 17 B. C., Agrippa's rôle was second only to that of Augustus.

It may be that Agrippa built a branch of the Euripus past the Tarentum and another in the direction of the Pons Agrippae. This newly discovered Euripus, in spite of its width of over ten feet and a depth of six feet can hardly have been the portion of Agrippa's Euripus in which Seneca took his annual New Year's plunge. If the recently discovered canal is to be connected with Agrippa at all, it must have been a branch outlet to the Tiber with possibly, as has been stated, another running in the direction of the Pons Agrippae. The Euripus itself, referred to by Ovid and Seneca in connection with the Stagnum and Horti, must have been a larger canal than this.

[100] Dio LIV, 29, see Appendix, p. 89; Ovid, *Ex Ponto*, I, 8, 37-38; *CIL*, VI, 29781; *Not. Scav.*, 1885, p. 343.

[101] Huelsen, *Top.*, I³, p. 580.

[102] See p. 25, n. 24.

[103] XIII, 1, 19 (p. 590), cited in Appendix, p. 90.

[104] For the references see p. 32, n. 86.

Sudatorium goes on to say: "Also he completed the building called the Pantheon. It has this name perhaps because it received among the images which decorated it the statues of many gods, including Mars and Venus; but my opinion is that, because of its vaulted roof[105] it resembles the heavens. Agrippa, for his part, wished to place a statue of Augustus there also, and to bestow upon him the honor of having the structure named after him; but when the emperor would not accept either honor, he placed in the temple itself a statue of the former Caesar and in the ante-room statues of Augustus and himself. This was done not out of any rivalry or ambition on Agrippa's part to make himself equal to Augustus, but from his hearty loyalty to him and his constant zeal for the country's good; hence Augustus, so far from censuring him for it, honored him the more."[106] This passage and the inscription[107] on the frieze of the pronaos: *M · Agrippa · L · f · cos · tertium · fecit,* seemed to justify the belief, which was generally held up to 1892, that, among the structures of Agrippa erected on the Campus Martius, the Pantheon presented fewest problems, and at least in its general lines was essentially the structure erected by Agrippa.[108] Since 1892 and the discoveries of Chedanne, to be described later, the Pantheon has been the subject of more controversies than all the other works of Agrippa put together. Let us first discuss the historical records in regard to Agrippa's building down to the time of its destruction in the fire of Titus in 80 A. D.[109]

From the inscription[110] it has generally been assumed that

[105] Dio was writing after the reconstruction by Hadrian. This opinion is clearly personal and may be based upon the temple as Dio saw it at the end of the second century. For the question as to whether Agrippa's original temple had a vaulted roof, see discussion on p. 60 and in n. 143.

[106] Dio LIII, 27, 2-4. The Greek text is given in the Appendix, p. 89.

[107] *CIL*, VI, 896.

[108] Lanciani, *R. and E.*, p. 477, sums up the consensus of opinion held at that time: (1) that the present Pantheon inscribed with the name of Agrippa was substantially his work; (2) that the portico was a later addition to, or alteration of, the original plan; (3) that some details of the structure, especially the inner decoration, were the work of Hadrian and of Severus and Caracalla; (4) that the Pantheon had never been used as a Caldarium (of the baths).

[109] Dio LXVI, 24, 2, cited in Appendix, p. 90.

[110] See n. 107. The bronze letters are modern, but set in the ancient sockets.

the Pantheon was completed in 27 B. C., the date of Agrippa's third consulship. But Dio,[111] who must have seen the inscription, states that it was completed in the ninth consulship of Augustus with M. Silanus as his colleague, that is to say in 25 B. C. Efforts have been made to harmonize these discordant statements by the assumption that the material completion took place in 27 B. C. and the formal dedication in 25 B. C.[112] But this reasoning is quite unnecessary. According to usual epigraphic custom the name of Agrippa would appear on inscriptions with the title *consul tertium* from 27 B. C. until his death.[113] The words *consul tertium* simply furnish the date after which. As Dio gives the consuls, Augustus consul for the ninth time, with M. Silanus as his colleague, and was no doubt using some such annalistic record as that of Livy, we may assume that his date for the completion of the Pantheon is correct.

Four other items in Dio's account deserve special comment. (1) It will be noted that the completion of the Pantheon took place in the same year as the completion of the first unit of the baths. Was there any integral connection between the two structures? This is discussed in n. 27. (2) Dio offers two explanations for the name Pantheon: (a) because it received among the statues which decorated it the statues of many gods, including Mars and Venus; (b) his own opinion that because of its vaulted roof it resembled the heavens. The second may be dismissed, since it is clear that Dio was assuming that Agrippa's structure had the same architectural features as those of Hadrian's reconstruction with which he was familiar. (3) Mars and Venus were included among the "many gods," and a statue of Julius Caesar was placed in the temple itself. Agrippa would have placed Augustus there also, had not the latter

[111] LIII, 27, 1, given in Appendix, p. 89. [112] Lanciani, *R. and E.*, p. 474.

[113] One need only cite the commemorative coins struck in the year of his death by Cossus and Lentulus, which have COS·TER·; or those struck in the reign of Tiberius which have COS · III · (*BMC, Coins of the Roman Empire*, Pl. 4, no. 12, Pl. 26, no. 7), or Frontinus, *de Aquis*, I, 10, who dates the building of the Aqua Virgo as follows: idem cum iam tertium consul fuisset, C. Sentio, Q. Lucretio consulibus (= 19 B. C.) . . . . Virginem quoque . . . . Romam perduxit.

protested. Whether Pantheon meant "many gods,"[114] or "all the gods,"[115] or "very holy,"[116] it was Agrippa's obvious intention to feature the *gens Iulia* and its divine ancestors. (4) Dio mentions that the statues of Augustus and Agrippa were placed in the pronaos. The two niches at each side of the entrance to the present Pantheon seem to have perpetuated this general arrangement after Hadrian's reconstruction, and Dio is probably describing what he saw in his own day.

The other references to Agrippa's Pantheon down to its destruction in the fire of Titus are surprisingly slight, when one considers that Virgil was writing his *Aeneid* and Horace the first three books of the *Odes* at the time of its dedication. Pliny[117] and Macrobius[118] mention the fact that the earrings of the statue of Venus were made of the two halves of a pearl which had belonged to Cleopatra. Pliny[119] states that some of the artistic decorations of the Pantheon were made by Diogenes of Athens, especially the Caryatids[120] *in columnis templi,* and the statues on the gable, which on account of the height at which they were placed were not so famous; also that the capitals of the columns were of Syracusan bronze.[121] Dio,[122] in connection with the events of B. C. 22, states that many objects in that year were struck by lightning, especially the statues in the Pantheon, so that the spear even fell from the hands of Augustus. Suetonius[123] mentions an omen occurring in 14 A. D., which Augustus interpreted as portending his approaching end. While he was performing the lustration in the Campus

[114] Rosch. III, 1555; Dar. Saglio IV, 315.

[115] Mommsen suggested the seven planetary divinities to correspond to the seven niches of the present Pantheon. But where could Julius Caesar have stood?

[116] Huelsen-Jordan, *Top.*, I³, p. 583.

[117] *N. H.*, IX, 121.

[118] III, 17, 17.

[119] *N. H.*, XXXVI, 38: Agrippae Pantheum decoravit Diogenes Atheniensis; in columnis templi eius Caryatides probantur inter pauca operum, sicut in fastigio posita signa, sed propter altitudinem loci minus celebrata.

[120] There is no place for these in the plan of Hadrian's reconstruction.

[121] *N. H.*, XXXIV, 13: Syracusana (aenea) sunt in Pantheo capita columnarum a M. Agrippa posita.

[122] LIV, 1, 1.

[123] *Aug.*, 97: Cum lustrum in Campo Martio magna populi frequentia conderet, aquila eum saepius circumvolavit transgressaque in vicinam aedem super nomen Agrippae ad primam litteram sedit.

Martius, in connection with the census of that year, an eagle circled about him several times and then flew to a neighboring temple and perched over the first letter of Agrippa's name. This temple with the name of Agrippa upon it was in all probability[124] the Pantheon, whose connection with the divinities of the *gens Iulia* we have already seen. In the *Acta Arvalia*[125] for the year 59 A. D. there is a statement that the brethren met *in Pantheo*, on January 12.

History records that Agrippa's Pantheon was destroyed in the fire of Titus along with the Serapeum and Iseum, the Saepta, the Basilica Neptuni, the Diribitorium, the theatre of Balbus, the stage building of Pompey's theatre, the Porticus Octaviae with its library, and the temple of Jupiter Capitolinus with its surrounding temples.[126] It was restored by Domitian.[127] It was struck by lightning again under Trajan in 110 A. D. and burned.[128] It is clear, therefore, that neither the original structure, nor Domitian's restoration, were fireproof, and that from this point of view the construction must have been radically different from that of the existing Pantheon. Hadrian restored it, along with several other buildings of Agrippa in this region: the Saepta, the Basilica Neptuni, and the Baths.[129] He also occasionally held court there.[130] That this restoration is represented by the existing Pantheon we shall see later, and it is probable that the mention made in Julius Capitolinus[131] of a restoration by Antoninus Pius refers to the completion of Hadrian's work. The last restoration in antiquity of which we have knowledge is that of Severus and

[124] Especially since Lundström has made it clear *(op. cit.)* that the letters *GRI* on the fragment of the Marble Plan (see Huelsen's map, fig. 2) have nothing to do with Agrippa, but that the name of the building to which they belonged was Porticus Melea*gri*. (See p. 66.)

[125] *CIL*, VI, 2041.

[126] Dio LXVI, 24, 1-2, cited in Appendix, p. 90.

[127] Hieron., an. Abr. 2105, mentions it last in a long list of constructions by that emperor. Cf. also *Chron. Min.*, p. 146.

[128] Orosius VII, 12: Pantheon Romae fulmine concrematum; cf. Hieron., an. Abr. 2127.

[129] *Vit. Hadr.*, 19, cited in Appendix, p. 92.

[130] Dio LXIX, 7, 1.

[131] *Vit. Antonin. Pii*, c. 8.

Caracalla, 202 A. D. The smaller inscription[132] on the architrave, below the Agrippa inscription, states, after the long list of titles of the two emperors: Pantheum vetustate corruptum cum omni cultu restituerunt. The last mention of the Pantheon in ancient literature is in *Cod. Theod.*, XIV, 3, 10: lecta in Pantheo Non. Nov. (368 or 370 A. D.).

What traces of Agrippa's Pantheon, either in the way of actual remains or of the original plan are to be found in the present Pantheon? We have seen that Agrippa's Pantheon, destroyed in the fire of Titus, cannot have been fire proof, and must have had a roof of wood. Had the roofed rotunda, 144 feet in diameter and of equal height, been a feature of the original building, Pliny and Dio would hardly have singled out Agrippa's Diribitorium for special mention on account of the size of its roof, and had its general dimensions been of the magnitude of the present Pantheon, it is hard to see how such an architectural marvel could have escaped the mention of contemporary Augustan writers. We have already seen that there is no place in the present plan for the Caryatids of the Athenian sculptor Diogenes. The original Pantheon may have been a structure of quite a different character from the present.

The startling discovery was made in 1892 by the French architect Chedanne[133] that the present rotunda was erected under Hadrian about the years 120-124 A. D., notwithstanding the evidence of the Agrippa inscription on the pronaos. Brick-stamps found in the dome, and later in the other parts of the rotunda, established this fact beyond a doubt. Chedanne's discoveries led to investigations by Beltrami[134] and Armanini in 1892-93, which have been followed more recently by the studies of Colini and Gismondi,[135] of Cozzo[136] about the same time, and finally the as yet unpublished studies which have been made by the architect Terenzio and his colleagues during the

[132] *CIL*, VI, 896.
[133] His results were not published.
[134] *Il Pantheon* (Milan, 1898).
[135] *Bull. Com.*, 1927, p. 67 ff.
[136] *Ingegneria Romana* (Rome, 1928).

recent thorough repairs on the structure.[137] Space will not permit more than a summary of their findings.[138] They are not always in agreement, so that the riddle of the sphinx of the Campus Martius is still in part unsolved.

Without going into the details of these differences of opinion, the main results as summarized by von Gerkan,[139] and in the new edition of Anderson and Spiers, *The Architecture of Ancient Rome,* revised by Thomas Ashby in 1927,[140] are as follows: The present domed rotunda, the octostyle portico, the rectangular projection[141] connecting the two, and also the rectangular hall to the south, formerly called the Laconicum, were the work of Hadrian's time. The so-called Grottoni, which connected the latter with the rotunda, also show stamps of Hadrian's time and must have been built as a reinforcement of the rotunda wall, on the south side, shortly after its erection. The restoration under Severus, already referred to, probably had to do with repairs which became necessary as the result of cracks which had developed, and may also have included the renewal of some of the interior decorative features.[142] If these views are correct, and they represent the consensus of opinion, no part of the present Pantheon can be ascribed to Agrippa,[143] and the inscription may be explained in the light of Hadrian's well-known policy, as stated by Aelius Spartianus, of not plac-

[137] There is a sketchy report by Carlo Montani in *Capitolium,* Sept., 1932.

[138] An excellent review is given by von Gerkan in *Gnomon,* 1929, p. 273 ff.

[139] *Op. cit.*

[140] Pp. 78-82.

[141] Colini and Gismondi, *op. cit.,* seem to have proven that the portico and the rectangular projection called by the Italian architects the "avancorpo," were built contemporaneously. Cozzo, *op. cit.,* agrees with this conclusion, but considered both to be later than the wall of the rotunda.

[142] Cozzo, *op. cit.,* ascribed to Severus the transfer of the portico with the Agrippa inscription to the north side of the Pantheon in the belief that it originally adjoined the large hall to the south, which in his opinion formed, as it were, an atrium to the Pantheon; he also believed that the portico originally dated from the time of Augustus. This theory was not confirmed in the recent repairs of the crack in the south axis, since the investigation revealed no entrance to the rotunda on that side.

[143] Cozzo apparently still held to the theory that the rotunda goes back to Agrippa, although the dome was of later construction, and that the superposition of the dome upon the rotunda caused the cracks to appear which made necessary the building of the structure known as the Grottoni to the south and also the rectangular projection on the north to support the rotunda wall, as it were, between the jaws of a vise, against the thrust of the dome.

ing his own name on a building which he either built or restored, except in the case of the temple of Trajan.[144]

Where then shall we look for the traces of Agrippa's Pantheon? In the excavations conducted under the present Pantheon, by Beltrami and Armanini, and later by Colini and Gismondi, there were found under the portico, at a depth of about 2.50 m., the walls of the podium of an oblong rectangular building, presumably a temple, with its pronaos projecting to the south from the long side of the rectangle, as in the case of the temple of Concord. The walls of the foundations were of travertine blocks, with rusticated facings. These foundations are usually identified as belonging to the Pantheon of Agrippa.[145] The dimensions of the building proper were 43.76 by 19.82 metres. On its north foundation wall (see Figure 3) rest the eight columns of the present portico, which has a width of 34 m. The earlier wall therefore extended 4.88 m. in each direction beyond the present row of columns. This gave rise to the theory of Chedanne, now disproved, that originally the portico was longer, and had ten columns instead of eight.[146] The width of the southward-facing pronaos of the older temple was 21.6 metres,[147] roughly half of the length of the long side of the rectangle from which it projected. This arrangement which, as we have seen, recalls that of the temple of Concord, also suggests the possibility that the pediment of the pronaos may have been supported by the Caryatids of Diogenes, mentioned by Pliny as a feature of Agrippa's temple, and that Agrippa, or his architect, may have been influenced by this feature of the Erectheum.

Some eight feet below the floor of the rotunda itself were found traces of the concrete bed of a marble pavement, which underlay the greater part of the area now covered by the ro-

[144] *Vit. Hadr.*, 19.

[145] At the southwest corner were found traces of an outer marble incrustation which von Gerkan *(op. cit.)* would ascribe to the restoration by Domitian.

[146] The studies of Colini, *op. cit.*, have shown that the slope of the present gable was original.

[147] Traces of its foundation were found under the stair-well of the present Pantheon to the west of the entrance.

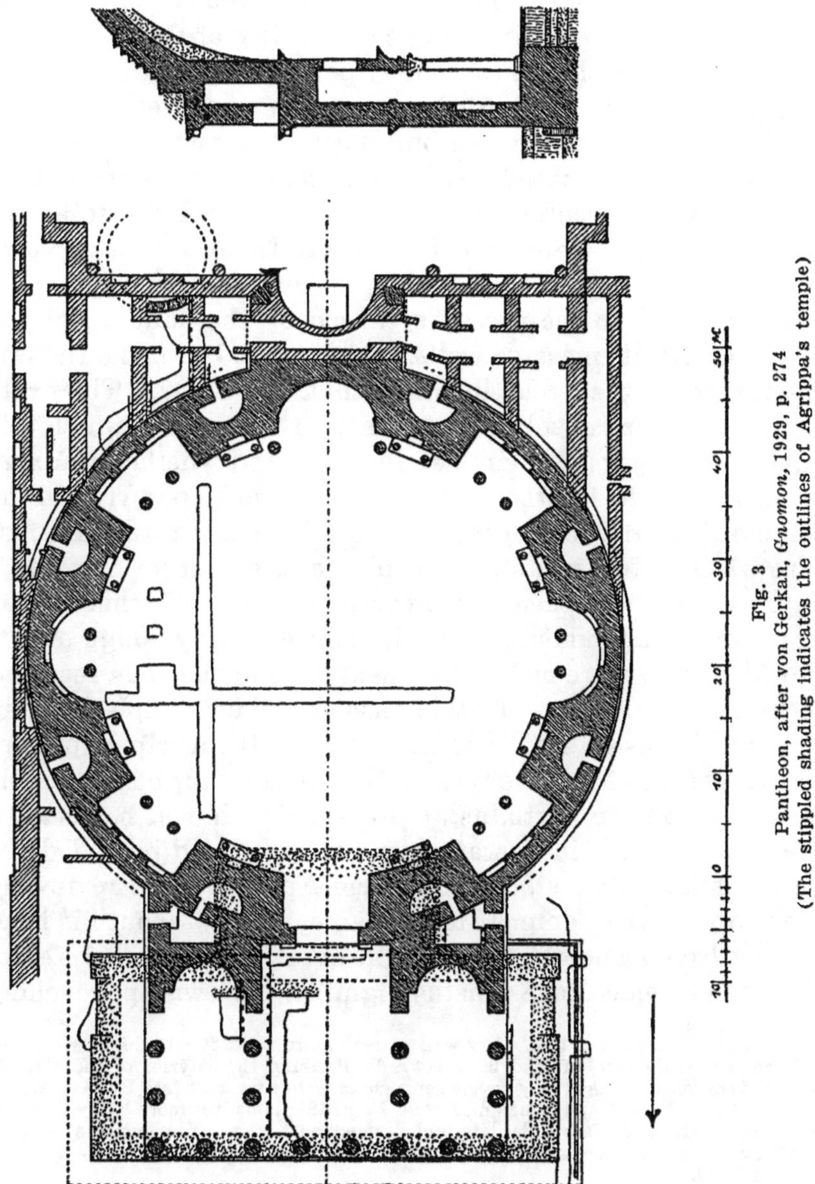

Fig. 3
Pantheon, after von Gerkan, *Gnomon*, 1929, p. 274
(The stippled shading indicates the outlines of Agrippa's temple)

tunda. Von Gerkan believes that this pavement, on account of objects found under it, belongs to the time of the restoration by Domitian, but that the area may perhaps go back to the time of Agrippa. The finding of this pavement raises two questions: (1) did it belong to a building; (2) or was it the pavement of an open piazza? The levels show that this pavement sloped from the center outward, which would indicate an attempt at drainage, and would therefore favor the latter view, but it is also possible that the sloping of the pavement may have been due to the pressure caused by the building of the rotunda with its massive walls, which tended to make the circumference of the circle sink more than the center. The problem still remains unsolved as to whether the area to which this pavement belongs was circular in shape and whether Hadrian in rebuilding the Pantheon after the fire, which occurred in the reign of Trajan, was reproducing in his domed rotunda a feature which dated, in its ground plan at least, from Agrippa's day. It may have been that this circular area, whether roofed or not, was surrounded by a wall, not necessarily a high one,[148] in which there were niches for the statues of the gods referred to by Dio Cassius.[149] In this case the older temple already referred to was entered from the area, and the Agrippa inscription must originally have been on the south façade of the temple instead of on the north, as at present.[150] It will be recalled that Suetonius,[151] in narrating the omens which preceded the death of Augustus, stated that when Augustus was reviewing the people in the Campus Martius an eagle flew about his head and settled on a neighboring temple over the letter *A* of Agrippa's name, which to Augustus signified his own approaching

[148] It has been surmised that a low wall of reticulate work 60 cm. thick, which can still be seen at the level of Hadrian's rotunda, flanking the exterior of the rotunda wall and concentric with it may have been such an enclosure wall (see Platner-Ashby, *Top. Dict.*, p. 385, n. 2, and Lanciani, *R. and E.*, p. 481), but it is more likely that this particular wall is of Hadrianic date and formed part of the foundation-system of the drum. (See von Gerkan, *op. cit.*, p. 276.)

[149] LIII, 27.

[150] Lundström, *op. cit.*, so believes, also Boethius in his review in *Gnomon*, 1931.

[151] See n. 123.

end. If this temple, as now seems probable,[152] was the Pantheon, then, in order for an inscription on the south façade to be visible from the Campus Martius, the walls of the enclosure of the circular area cannot have been of any great height.

We are concerned in this article primarily with the building operations of Agrippa. The Pantheon, as rebuilt by Hadrian, though now despoiled of its gilded roof, the gilded rosettes of the coffers of the ceiling of the dome, the marble decorations of the attic story removed in 1747, and the bronze trusses (450,-251 pounds in weight) supporting the roof of the portico which Urban VIII caused to be melted up to cast cannon for Castel S. Angelo, is still one of the architectural marvels of the world, the starting point of the studies of all the great fifteenth and sixteenth century architects. Its construction, apparently so simple, is most complex, even to the professional architect. It forms a subject by itself, which can best be studied in some recent work amply illustrated by plans, sections, and details of construction, such as Rivoira's *Roman Architecture,* 1925, or Anderson, Spiers, Ashby, *The Architecture of Ancient Rome,* 1927.

Sepulcrum Agrippae

Somewhere in the Campus Martius, and probably in Region IX, was located the tomb which Agrippa had intended for himself, but which remained so far as he was concerned a mere cenotaph, since we are informed by Dio[153] that Augustus buried Agrippa in his own mausoleum, although Agrippa had taken one for himself in the Campus Martius. Huelsen[154] believed that this tomb of Agrippa was the *vicina aedes* on which the eagle perched over the first letter of the name of Agrippa on the occasion of the omen already mentioned on p. 64, which to Augustus portended his own approaching end. He further

[152] See below under Sepulcrum Agrippae.
[153] LIV, 28, 5.
[154] *Top.*, I³, p. 572, also Taf. X (facing p. 568).

thought that fragments 103 and 72 of the Marble Plan, which, as put together by him, yield the letters

M . . . . GRI
. . . VLI . . .

represented two tombs (1) sepulchru]m or monumentu]m [A]gri[ppae] and (2) monumentum I]uli [orum]. These tombs, he thought, lay between the Thermae Agrippae and the Villa Publica because of the letters PUBLIC on another fragment (97) of the Marble Plan. On his map (see Figure 2) he has inserted the main fragment a little to the southwest of the Serapeum. But this explanation has been set at naught by the masterful solving of the puzzle by Lundström[155] who has fitted in still another fragment (frag. 95), preserved only in a drawing, and has shown that the two monuments were PORTIC[US] M[ELEA]GRI and AE[DES I]VLI[ORUM]. We must therefore look elsewhere in the Campus Martius for Agrippa's tomb.

The Pons Agrippae

To the numerous building activities of Agrippa in the Campus Martius we may add a Pons Agrippae which crossed the Tiber a short distance above the later Pons Aurelius, the present Ponte Sisto. We owe our knowledge of the existence of this Pons Agrippae entirely to a *cippus*[156] set up by the *curatores riparum* in the reign of Claudius which states that they had regulated the Tiber bank and placed such *cippi* "a Trigario ad Pontem Agrippae." Borsari[157] identified this bridge with four piers discovered in the bed of the river, 102 metres above the axis of the Ponte Sisto, on the east bank, and 132 m. above it on the west bank. The location of the tomb of Platorinus, which belongs to the Augustan Age, shows that at that period a street ran from the western bridge-head

[155] See n. 42.

[156] *CIL*, VI, 31545. This *cippus* was found in 1877, behind the Church of S. Biagio della Pagnotta, near the Strada Giulia.

[157] *Not. Scav.*, 1887, p. 323. See *Bull. Com.*, 1888, pp. 92-98, Pls. IV and V; also Lanciani, *R. and E.*, pp. 21-22.

towards the Janiculum. The bridge, if it had not already been damaged by floods, was apparently torn down when Caracalla built the Pons Aurelius, and perhaps its materials were used in the construction of the later bridge. A change of angle of 20° between the axis of the Pons Agrippae and the Pons Aurelius indicates that the course of the river had also been changed.

A clue as to the occasion and the probable date of the building of the bridge, which seems to have escaped the notice of the topographers, is furnished by a statement of Frontinus in regard to the Aqua Virgo, which Agrippa built in 19 B. C. He says that that aqueduct served Regions VII, IX, and XIV.[158] Now the Fourteenth Region is across the river from Region Nine, and, if the aqueduct as built by Agrippa originally served the Trastevere quarter, its conduit must have been carried over the Tiber on a bridge, and as the inscription testifies to the fact that Agrippa built a bridge, we may assume that this bridge carried his aqueduct, and that the two were probably contemporaneous. We have seen in the previous paragraph that a street ran from the western bridge-head to the Janiculum in Augustan times, and presumably the bridge carried a road as well as the conduit of the Virgo, as in the case of the Pont du Gard near Nîmes. As the level of the Virgo was the lowest of all the aqueducts, except the Appia and the Alsietina,[159] the conduit cannot have been much higher than the parapet of the bridge itself. The water of the Alsietina which Augustus built to serve his naumachia in Region XIV, in 2 B. C., was according to Frontinus not suitable for drinking. The construction of the Aqua Traiana in 109 A. D., not long after Frontinus wrote his work on the aqueducts, must have made the supply from the Virgo superfluous from that time on, so that when Caracalla built the Pons Aurelius, the present Ponte Sisto, a short distance below the site of the now dismantled Pons Agrippae, there was no need for it to carry the conduit of the Virgo.

[158] *De Aquis*, II, 84. See also p. 33, n. 94.

[159] Frontin., *de Aquis*, I, 18.

Three other structures in Region IX have been assigned to Agrippa by individual topographers, either erroneously or without sufficient evidence.

Lanciani on p. 443 of *Ruins and Excavations of Ancient Rome* erroneously lists the Villa Publica among Agrippa's buildings, although on p. 472 of the same work he states that it was rebuilt by P. Fonteius Capito.

Lanciani also lists among the works of Agrippa the Porticus Eventus Boni.[160] This porticus and the temple from which it got its name are mentioned only once in literature. Ammianus Marcellinus[161] states that Claudius, Prefect of the city in 374 A. D., restored many ancient structures and reared a huge portico adjoining the baths of Agrippa, which portico was named Eventus Boni after a temple of that divinity near by. Five large capitals of white marble, 1.70 metres high, which were found between the present church of S. Maria in Monterone and the Theatro Valle, may belong to the porticus and thus mark its position.[162] Sarti[163] would identify the temple itself with some ancient peperino walls on the site of S. Maria in Monterone.[164] Platner-Ashby suggests that the temple may have been one of the buildings of Agrippa.[165] But there is no real evidence to connect either the portico or the temple with Agrippa except their proximity to his Thermae. As for the portico, it would appear from the context in Ammianus that this was a new structure and not a restoration.

[160] *Ruins and Excavations*, pp. 443, 445.

[161] XXIX, 6, 17: instauravit vetera plurima, inter quae porticum excitavit ingentem lavacro Agrippae contiguam, Eventus Boni cognominatam, ea quod huius numinis prope visitur templum.

[162] Platner-Ashby, *Top. Dict.*, p. 420.

[163] *Arch. d. Soc. Rom. di Storia Patria*, IX, 476.

[164] See map in fig. 2; also Huelsen, *Top.*, I³, p. 581; *Thermen des Agrippa*, pp. 33-34.

[165] *Top. Dict.*, p. 86.

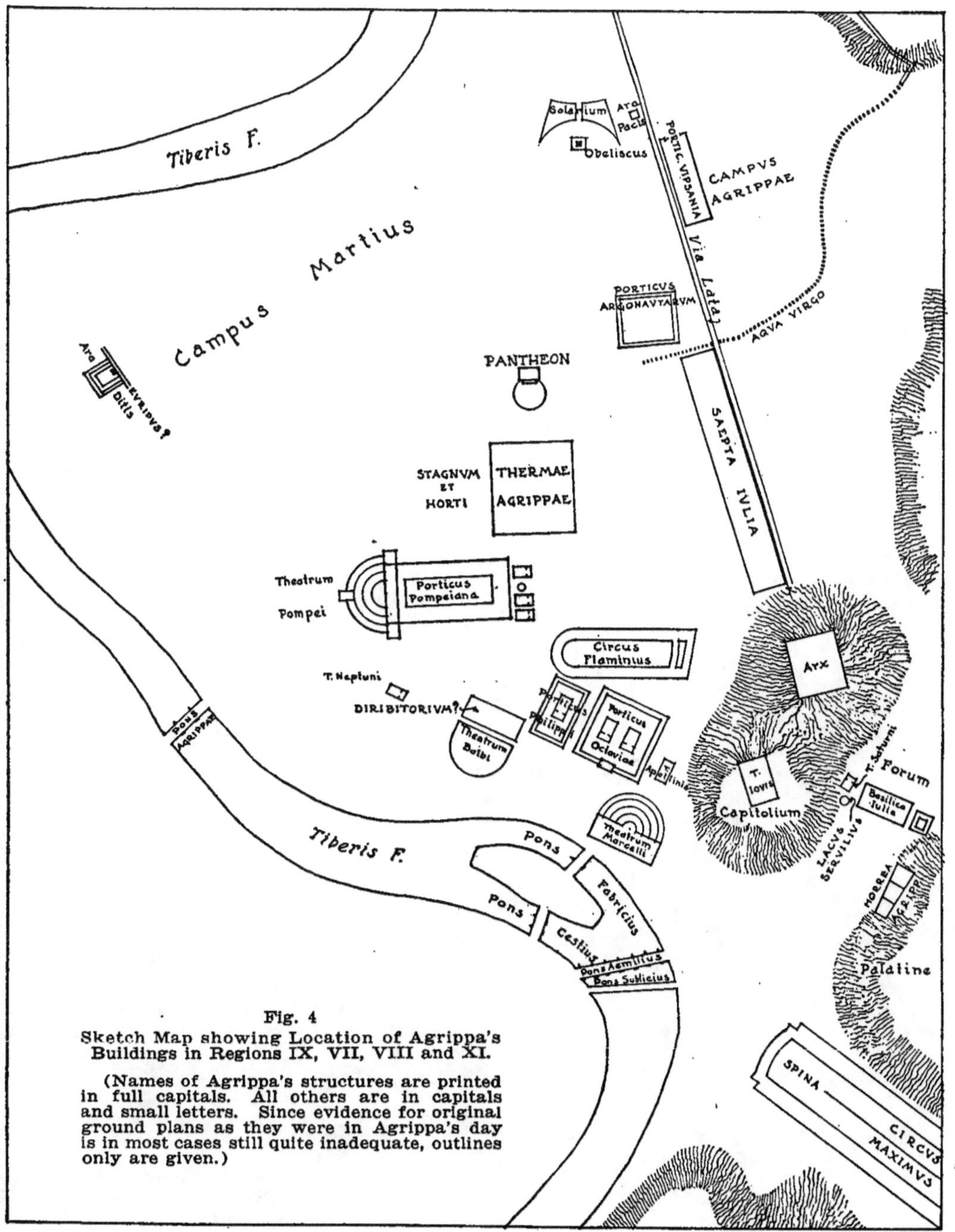

Fig. 4
Sketch Map showing Location of Agrippa's Buildings in Regions IX, VII, VIII and XI.

(Names of Agrippa's structures are printed in full capitals. All others are in capitals and small letters. Since evidence for original ground plans as they were in Agrippa's day is in most cases still quite inadequate, outlines only are given.)

GROUP III

THE CAMPUS AGRIPPAE AND THE PORTICUS VIPSANIA IN REGION VII

Group III

THE CAMPUS AGRIPPAE AND THE PORTICUS VIPSANIA IN REGION VII

As early as 19 B. C. Agrippa had constructed the Aqua Virgo across Region VII. This ran along the edge of the Pincian Hill, turned southwest near the Via Capo le Case, where it emerged and began to run on arches for the remaining 700 paces of its course. Just before crossing the modern Via del Tritone it turned southwest by south to the modern Piazzi di Trevi, and thence a little south of west to the Via Flaminia, which it crossed, and ended a short distance beyond the northern end of the Saepta. In the area bounded on the east and south by the arches of the aqueduct and on the west by the Via Flaminia the topographers locate the Campus Agrippae, and along the Via Flaminia the Porticus Vipsania which housed the famous map of Agrippa. We have references to both, but none which assign a definite date for either of them within the life of Agrippa. We have definite information that the Porticus Vipsania was not finished until more than five years after his death. Both present certain problems. Was the aqueduct the eastern limit of the Campus, or did the Campus extend beyond it? What were its northern limits? How far north did the Porticus Vipsania extend? Do the references in Martial, in which he uses the adjective *Vipsanius,* refer to the Portico or to the Campus, or were the two regarded as a single group, covered in Martial's mind by a single name? Do his frequent references to Europa refer to a painting in the Porticus, or to a statuary group in the gardens of the Campus? These problems will be discussed under the separate heads.

Campus Agrippae

Dio states,[1] among the events of the year 7 B. C., that τὸ πεδίον τὸ Ἀγρίππειον was made public property by Augustus,

[1] LV, 8, 3-4. The Greek text is quoted in full in Appendix, p. 90. It will be there noted that in the first sentence he says πλὴν τῆς στοᾶς and in the last sentence

but that the portico located upon it (i. e. the Porticus Vipsania) was not included. Gellius mentions the Campus Agrippae as the scene of the conversation which took place in *N. A.* XIV, 5.[2] It is listed in the *Curiosum* and the *Notitia*[3] under Regio VII, Via Lata, along with the Porticus Gypsiani or Gyptiani, which is no doubt a corruption of Vipsanii or Vipsania. We have no other mention of it by name in ancient sources except for a statement that Aurelian *castra in campo Agrippae dedicavit.*[4] It was evidently laid out as a park, and the reference in Gellius already quoted shows that it was a favorite promenade. While we have no reference to it by name it is not improbable that numerous passages in Martial have to do with the park rather than with the Porticus Vipsania with which they have been ordinarily associated. The *Vipsaniae laurus*[5] on which his lodgings looked, certainly suggest a park rather than a portico, and the adjective may mean nothing more than *Agrippianae,* or *Agrippae.*[6] Poets are given to suggestive rather than literal terms. Four[7] of the epigrams, in which he is referring to favorite haunts, contain the name of Europa, under various guises. Huelsen assumed that this was a painting in the Porticus Vipsania, and was used by Martial to designate that Portico. But the expressions *Europes tepida buxeta,*[8] and *An delicatae sole rursus Europae, inter tepentes post meridiem buxos*[9] clearly refer to a park or gardens, and, if they are to be

ἡ ἐν τῷ πεδίῳ στοά, showing that the Porticus stood on the Campus, but was not included at this time in the gift to the people, either because it was not finished or because it was built by Agrippa's sister and did not come under the property which Augustus had inherited from Agrippa.

[2] Defessus ego quondam diutina commentatione laxandi levandique animi gratia in Agrippae Campo deambulabam. Atque ibi duos forte grammaticos conspicatus, etc.

[3] See Appendix, p. 92.

[4] Chronogr. an. 354 in *Mon. Germ. Hist.*, IX, p. 148.

[5] I, 108, 3.

[6] It may be that the *Vipsanis Columnis* of Mart., IV, 18, 1-2 (Qua vicina pluit Vipsanis porta columnis / Et madet assiduo lubricus imbre lapis) refer to Agrippa's *nomen* rather than to that of his sister, in view of the fact that the excavations in the Piazza Colonna make it necessary to move the supposed location of the Porticus Vipsania north to 7 metres south of the Via del Tritone, a considerable distance from the aqueduct. See p. 76, n. 23.

[7] Mart., II, 14; lines 3 and 15; III, 20, 12; VII, 32, 11-12; XI, 1, 10.

[8] II, 14, 15.

[9] III, 20, 12-13.

connected with Agrippa at all, must refer to the Campus. In this case the Europa must have been a sculptured group[10] standing in the park, rather than a painting.

As has been already stated the limits of the Campus Agrippae to the north are uncertain, and there is also a question as to whether it extended eastward beyond the arches of the Aqua Virgo up the valley between the Quirinal and the Pincian Hills. Becker,[11] and after him Huelsen,[12] thought that the Campus Agrippae was *τὸ ἄλλο πεδίον* of the famous description of Rome in Strabo.[13] But the identification does not seem possible. The mention of three theatres, an amphitheatre, costly temples in close succession, as well as the colonnades all round about it, makes it much more likely that Strabo is there describing the region of the Circus Flaminius. Armini[14] identifies that part of the Campus Martius which lay east of the Via Flaminia, in which the Campus Agrippae was later laid out, as the Campus Minor of Catullus.[15]

Porticus Vipsania

The chief source of our information in regard to this portico is the passage of Dio already cited,[16] in which he states that in 7 B. C. Augustus made the Campus Agrippae, with the exception of the Porticus, public property, and then goes on to say in the same connection that "the portico in the Campus (*sc.* Agrippae) which was being built by Polla, Agrippa's sister, who also adorned the race-courses, was not yet finished." Pliny,[17] in connection with the world-map of Agrippa, which

[10] A. Reinach, *Neapolis,* II, 1915, pp. 231-253, attempts to show that this was a group by Pythagoras brought from Tarentum.

[11] P. 597.

[12] Jordan-Huelsen, I^3, p. 458.

[13] V, 3, 8, cited in Appendix, p. 90.

[14] *Eranos,* 1923, pp. 53-54.

[15] 53, 3. Te in Campo quaesivinus Minore
Te in Circo, te in omnibus libellis.

[16] LV, 8, 3-4. See Appendix, p. 90.

[17] *N. H.,* III, 17: Agrippa quidem in tanta viri diligentia praeterque in hoc opere (the map) cura, cum orbi terrarum spectandum propositurus esset, errasse quis eum credat et cum eo divum Augustum? Is namque complexam eum porticum ex destinatione et commentariis M. Agrippae a sorore eius incohatam peregit.

was set up in this portico, states that the portico was begun by Agrippa's sister in accordance with the purpose and the will of Agrippa, and was completed by Augustus. The name of the portico, corrupted in the manuscripts to *Vipsanda,* or *inspanda,* is found in another passage [18] of the same author. It is mentioned by Tacitus[19] and Plutarch[20] in connection with the events of 69 A. D., as the place where detachments of the Illyrian Army were quartered. It is also listed along with the Campus Agrippae in the *Notitia,* Reg. VII,[21] where the name had been corrupted to *Porticus Gypsiani.* From a passage in Martial,[22] it was formerly supposed that it extended along the Via Flaminia nearly as far south as the Aqua Virgo, but the excavations of 1914-16, opposite the Piazza Colonna, seem to show that the remains of a colonnade, extending only 7 metres south of the Via del Tritone, was the southern limit of the portico.[23] Its northern limit has not yet been determined, although remains conforming to the same plan were found in excavating for the Palazzo Bocconi.[24] The width of the colonnade, as disclosed by the excavation of the southern end in 1914-16, exceeded 43 m., of which 33 m. comprising the eastern end were excavated, disclosing seven bases for pilasters averaging 3 m. apart. The *Vipsanis Columnis* of Martial, as already suggested,[25] may refer to some smaller monument in the Campus Agrippae, near the Aqua Virgo, but associated in the poet's[26] mind with Agrippa himself, and not with his sister.

Mention has already[27] been made of the fact that Becker and Huelsen thought that numerous references to *Europa* in Martial had to do with a painting in the Porticus Vipsania. As two of them clearly describe a park, and are hardly applicable to a portico, the references must apply to the Campus Agrippae

[18] Plin., *N. H.*, VI, 139.

[19] *Hist.*, I, 31.

[20] *Galba*, 25.

[21] See Appendix, p. 92.

[22] Cited on p. 74, n. 6.

[23] *Bull. Com.*, 1914, p. 209; 1915, p. 218; and particularly 1917, p. 220; *Not. Scav.*, 1915, p. 35; 1917, pp. 9-20.

[24] Cantarelli, *Bull. Com.*, 1917, p. 220; *Not. Scav.*, 1917, p. 16.

[25] P. 74, n. 6.

[26] See p. 74, n. 6.

[27] See p. 74.

and not to the portico, if indeed Europa is to be associated with this region at all.

This portico, with its still more important map,[28] the plans for which were carried on by Agrippa's sister and completed by Augustus, formed a fitting monument to the self-effacing adjutant of the emperor, who both in works of war and of peace ranks second only to Augustus himself as a builder of the empire.

It was his original project to display to the Romans, and visitors to Rome, on a huge scale and in a special building, the known world of which the Roman Empire formed so large a part. His own official duties, first as general, and subsequently as co-regent with Augustus, had taken him from one end of the empire to the other, from Sinope in the east to the Cantabri in the west, and north into Gaul, where he was the second Roman general to cross the Rhine with an army, and to Pannonia, whence he returned to die. The map and the portico built to house it became in a sense a fitting symbol of his life.

Agrippa was *par excellence* a practical man, and the map probably served practical rather than scientific ends. Its measuring rods were no doubt the milestones of the Roman roads rather than latitude and longitude. We have no information as to whether the map was cut in the marble of a wall, or in the pavement of the portico. We can only exercise conjecture as to what the ποικίλματα were, which are mentioned by Strabo[29] who evidently saw it about 7 B. C., and whether the distances which Pliny so often quotes from Agrippa were cut in the stone as appendices to the map itself, or were taken from a book of *commentarii* prepared by Agrippa to supplement the map.[30]

[28] For the map and its relation to the portico, see p. 75, and for the references to it in Pliny, *N. H.*, see notes 17 and 18.

[29] II, 5, 17. See Appendix, p. 90.

[30] For the map, see especially Detlefsen, *Ursprung, Einrichtung und Bedeutung der Erdcarte Agrippas* (Berlin, 1906). For the extensive literature on the subject see Schanz, *Gesch. Roem. Litt., Müllers Handbuch,* VIII, ii, pt. 1 (1911), p. 459. In *Klio,* 1931, pp. 38-58, 386-466, the *Commentarii* have received exhaustive treatment from Alfred Klotz.

GROUP IV

THE HORREA AGRIPPIANA (Reg. VIII); THE HYDRA OF THE LACUS SERVILIUS (Reg. VIII); DECORATIONS OF THE CIRCUS (Reg. XI)

Group IV

THE HORREA AGRIPPIANA (Reg. VIII); THE HYDRA OF THE LACUS SERVILIUS (Reg. VIII); DECORATIONS OF THE CIRCUS (Reg. XI)

Horrea Agrippiana

A series of warehouses situated at the foot of the Palatine Hill along its northwestern edge, between the Clivus Victoriae and the Vicus Tuscus, which were partially excavated by Boni in 1904 and again in 1912, were presumably[1] the work of Agrippa, and along with the sewers and aqueducts bear witness to his penchant for erecting structures of a semipublic and utilitarian nature. Bartoli believes that they were connected with the administration of the *Annona.*[2]

The name Horrea Agrippiana appears on three inscriptions,[3] one of which was found in the excavations, and possibly on a fourth.[4] It also occurs in the *Curiosum,*[5] under Region VIII.

[1] There is no specific evidence, as in the case of his more pretentious buildings, connecting them with the name of Agrippa. But in the light of the inscriptions cited in n. 3, and the analysis of Bartoli, (see n. 2), there is really little doubt that these warehouses were either built by Agrippa or named in his honor.

[2] *Mon. Antich.*, 27, 1921, p. 398. He bases his conclusion upon the fact that the inscription upon the marble base found in the excavations (see n. 3), records the fact that the three dedicators call themselves *immunes.* This *immunitas* was the privilege of *negotiatores qui annonam urbis adiuvant* (*Dig.*, L, 6, 3). Schneider-Graziosi, *Bull. Com.*, 1914, 25-33 takes the same view.

[3] *CIL,* VI, 9972; 10026, apparently of the first century, are sepulchral inscriptions of persons who are called *vestiarii de horreis Agrippianis.* The third of these inscriptions, found in the excavations on the base of a statue to the Genius of the Horrea Agrippiana (Cf. Bartoli, *op. cit.*, p. 379), reads as follows: (Pro) salut · Genium · horreor / (A) grippianorum · negotiantib / L · Arrius · Hermes / C · Varius · Polycarpus / C · Paconius · Chrysanthus / immunes s · p · d · d. On the side of the same base appear the words: posit · dedic · V · Idus · Iun / Cn · Cossutio · Eustropho / L · Manlio · Philadelpho, and to the right of these two names: Cur · ann · III.

[4] *CIL,* XIV, 3958, a sepulchral inscription found at Nomentum, of a certain *vestiarius de horreis Agrippinianis.* The fact that, as in the case of the first two inscriptions cited in the previous note, it refers to a *vestiarius* might suggest that *Agrippinianis* may simply be a slip of the stone-cutter. But it is also possible that Horrea, of which we know nothing, may have been erected by one of the two Agrippinas.

[5] In the *Notitia* we find *Horrea Germaniciana et Agrippiana.* Bartoli, *loc. cit.*, p. 382 (see n. 2), has shown, by citing 82 examples in the *Curiosum* and the *Notitia,*

It is represented, though not by name, on the fragments of the Marble Plan of Septimius Severus[6] as having three units built around three courtyards, and lying between the Clivus Victoriae and the Vicus Tuscus, which are named in the plan. These courtyards are trapezoidal in shape to conform to the gradual converging of these two streets. The largest and most northerly of these units, lying between the church of S. Teodoro and the so-called Temple of Augustus, has been excavated and identified both by the plan, and by the inscription bearing the name.[7]

The trapezoidal court of the excavated portion was originally an open area, paved with slabs of travertine. This open area was surrounded by a portico of two or more stories, behind which were rectangular chambers, whose walls were built, at least on the first story, of tufa *(opus quadratum)*.[8] The space between the pilasters of the portico was half the width of each cella. The back wall on the north side was originally of *opus quadratum*, but was reconstructed in brickwork by Domitian when he erected or rebuilt the so-called Temple of Augustus. The court at a later date was filled with constructions of various periods.[9] Brick pillars were first built to support awnings. The chapel which contained the statue of the Genius Horreorum Agrippianorum was erected in the second century or third, as is shown by the style of its mosaic floor. Still later,

that there was a tendency to group different structures of the same type under one heading, and that the *Notitia* was probably grouping two different Horrea located in Reg. VIII, and points to the fact that the inscriptions show simply Horrea Agrippiana. Huelsen, *Forum Romanum*, p. 169, gives the double name: *Germaniciana et Agrippiana.* In the *Forum und Palatin*, p. 51, and also in the English èdition he calls the building simply *Horrea Germaniciana.* In both he seems to have made a strange slip. Referring to the inscription on the marble base found in the court he says: "In einer dieser Hoefe . . . ist eine Marmorbasis gefunden, welche den Namen des Gebaudes Horrea Germaniciana nennt: er weisst auf ihre Grundung durch Germanicus in der Zeit des Augustus oder Tiberius." The inscription, which we have given in n. 3, says distinctly *Genium horreor* (A) *grippianorum.*

[6] Fragments 37 and 86. Lanciani, *Bull. Com.*, 1885, pp. 157-160, was the first to identify the structure there represented with the Horrea Agrippiana.

[7] Cited in n. 3.

[8] For a ground plan see *Mon. Antich.*, 27, 1921, pp. 274-402, also Pls. I and II.

[9] Platner-Ashby, p. 260.

after the fourth century, as is shown by an inscribed stone which was used as building material, the courtyard was completely occupied by medieval structures, which were, however, arranged with reference to the pilasters of the portico. This fact led Bartoli[10] to believe that it continued to be used by the Byzantine and Gothic governments and even by the Church, after the building of S. Teodoro in the centre of the three courtyards, for the administration of the *Annona*.[11]

The Hydra of the Lacus Servilius

Strabo,[12] in his famous description of contemporary Rome, mentions the copious fountains (κρουνοὺς ἀφθόνους) with which, he adds, Agrippa especially concerned himself though he also adorned the city with many other structures. Pliny[13] states that within the single year of his aedileship (33 B. C.) Agrippa constructed 700 *lacus,* 500 *salientes,* and 300 *castella* (i. e., of the aqueducts), and on these works he placed 300 statues of marble or bronze, and 400 marble columns. Of these numerous fountains we have specific mention of only one.[14] We are indebted to Festus (290) for the statement[15] that Agrippa adorned the Lacus Servilius, at the head of the Vicus Jugarius and near the Basilica Julia, by placing upon it the figure of a hydra, presumably because the hydra, with its multiplicity of heads, lent itself readily to a fountain of many jets. The Lacus Servilius was already in existence in the time of Sulla, as we

[10] *Op. cit.*, pp. 398-402.

[11] For works dealing with the Horrea Agrippiana other than those mentioned in the notes see: Huelsen-Carter, *The Forum and Palatine,* p. 192; *Bull. Com.*, 1911, 158-172; *Mitt.*, 1905, 84; 1925, 213-214; *Year's Work,* 1915, 1-2; Paully-Wissowa, VIII, 2461.

[12] V, 3, 8. See Appendix, p. 90.

[13] *N. H.*, XXXVI, 121. See Appendix, p. 91. He may be wrong in including all these structures within the compass of a single year. In the same passage he is certainly wrong in placing the Aqua Virgo in the aedileship of Agrippa. See discussion on p. 26.

[14] Unless Martial, IV, 18, 1, *Qua vicina pluit Vipsanis porta columnis,* is referring to an ornamental fountain and not to the Porticus Vipsania, as is usually thought. See p. 74, n. 6.

[15] Servilius lacus appellabatur ab eo qui eum faciendum curaverat in principio vici Iugari, continens basilicae Juliae; in quo loco fuit effigies hydrae posita a M. Agrippa.

know from references to it in Cicero[16] and Seneca[17] referring to the proscriptions. Remains of this republican Lacus Servilius are thought,[18] though without certainty, to have been found under the imperial pavement of the Vicus Jugarius. These remains are of brown Anio stone, and measure 5 by 11 metres.[19] If this identification is correct, and, as stated in Platner-Ashby,[20] it was destroyed at the time of the restoration[21] of the temple of Saturn by Plancus (*circ.* 42 B. C.), it must have been moved at that time, or by Agrippa, to a near-by site.

The Dolphins and Ova on the Spina of the Circus

We have seen that Dio[22] in recording the acts of Agrippa during his aedileship in 33 B. C. states that he set up in the circus dolphins and egg-shaped devices to mark the laps of the races. This item seems inconsequential among his more important works. Dio probably excerpted it from a more extensive account of what Agrippa had done in connection with the games of the circus. Agrippa appears to have been interested in racing. At the Ludi Saeculares in 17 B. C. it was he who conducted the races of *quadrigae.*[23] Names of his freedmen[24] occur in a list of jockeys on an inscription of the *familia quadrigaria* of T. Ateius Capito, indicating that at some time in his life Agrippa probably owned a racing stable. We have a statement of Dio,[25] that his sister also decorated the race courses.

[16] *Pro. Rosc. Amerin.*, 32, 89: Multos caesos non ad Trasumenum sed ad Servilium lacum.

[17] *De Provid.*, 3, 7: videant largum in foro sanguinem et supra Servilianum lacum (id enim proscriptionis Sullanae spoliarium est) senatorum capita.

[18] Van Deman, *Jour. Rom. Stud.*, 1922, pp. 25-26.

[19] Frank, *Rom. Build. Rep.*, pp. 75-76.

[20] P. 314.

[21] The concrete of the foundation rests partly upon it. Van Deman, *loc. cit.*

[22] XLIX, 43, 2: "And seeing that in the circus men made mistakes about the number of laps completed he set up dolphins and egg-shaped objects (ᾠοειδῆ δημιουργήματα), so that by their aid the number of times the course had been circled might be clearly shown." The Greek text is given in Appendix, p. 89.

[23] *Act. Lud. Saec.*, line 65: M. Agrippa quadrigas misit.

[24] *CIL*, VI, 10046. The names are M. Vipsanius Migio, M. Vipsanius Calamus, M. Vipsanius Dareus, M. Vipsanius Faustus.

[25] LV, 8, 4. See Appendix, p. 90.

The dolphins no doubt suggested to the spectators Agrippa's naval victories over Sextus Pompey at Mylae and Naulochus. As to the *ova,* we have the statement of Livy[26] that they were first set up in 174 B. C.

[26] XLII, 27.

APPENDIX

APPENDIX

This appendix contains the text of the more lengthy passages from Greek and Latin authors, and also those which are cited more than once.

1. Greek Sources

Dio Cassius

XLIX, 43 (Agrippa's ædileship)

Τῷ δ' ὑστέρῳ ἔτει ἀγορανόμος ὁ Ἀγρίππας ἑκὼν ἐγένετο, καὶ πάντα μὲν τὰ οἰκοδομήματα τὰ κοινὰ πάσας δὲ τὰς ὁδούς, μηδὲν ἐκ τοῦ δημοσίου λαβών, ἐπεσκεύασε, τούς τε ὑπονόμους ἐξεκάθηρε, καὶ ἐς τὸν Τίβεριν δι' αὐτῶν ὑπέπλευσε. κἀν τῷ ἱπποδρόμῳ σφαλλομένους τοὺς ἀνθρώπους περὶ τὸν τῶν διαύλων ἀριθμὸν ὁρῶν τούς τε δελφῖνας καὶ τὰ ᾠοειδῆ δημιουργήματα κατεστήσατο, ὅπως δι' αὐτῶν αἱ περίοδοι τῶν περιδρόμων ἀναδεικνύωνται.

LIII, 27 (The Basilica of Neptune, the Laconicum Sudatorium, and the Pantheon)

Αὔγουστος μὲν ταῦτά τε ἐν τοῖς πολέμοις ἔπραξε, καὶ τὸ τοῦ Ἰανοῦ τεμένισμα ἀνοιχθὲν δι' αὐτοὺς ἔκλεισεν, Ἀγρίππας δὲ ἐν τούτῳ τὸ ἄστυ τοῖς ἰδίοις τέλεσιν ἐπεκόσμησε. τοῦτο μὲν γὰρ τὴν στοὰν τὴν τοῦ Ποσειδῶνος ὠνομασμένην καὶ ἐξῳκοδόμησεν ἐπὶ ταῖς ναυκρατίαις καὶ τῇ τῶν Ἀργοναυτῶν γραφῇ ἐπελάμπρυνε, τοῦτο δὲ τὸ πυριατήριον τὸ Λακωνικὸν κατεσκεύασε. Λακωνικὸν γὰρ τὸ γυμνάσιον, ἐπειδήπερ οἱ Λακεδαιμόνιοι γυμνοῦσθαί τε ἐν τῷ τότε χρόνῳ καὶ λίπα ἀσκεῖν μάλιστα ἐδόκουν, ἐπεκάλεσε. τό τε Πάνθειον ὠνομασμένον ἐξετέλεσε· προσαγορεύεται δὲ οὕτω τάχα μὲν ὅτι πολλῶν θεῶν εἰκόνας ἐν τοῖς ἀγάλμασι, τῷ τε τοῦ Ἄρεως καὶ τῷ τῆς Ἀφροδίτης, ἔλαβεν, ὡς δὲ ἐγὼ νομίζω, ὅτι θολοειδὲς ὂν τῷ οὐρανῷ προσέοικεν. ἠβουλήθη μὲν οὖν ὁ Ἀγρίππας καὶ τὸν Αὔγουστον ἐνταῦθα ἱδρῦσαι, τήν τε τοῦ ἔργου ἐπίκλησιν αὐτῷ δοῦναι· μὴ δεξαμένου δὲ αὐτοῦ μηδέτερον ἐκεῖ μὲν τοῦ προτέρου Καίσαρος, ἐν δὲ τῷ προνάῳ τοῦ τε Αὐγούστου καὶ ἑαυτοῦ ἀνδριάντας ἔστησε.

LIV, 29, 4 (The Gardens and Baths)

καὶ τότε γοῦν κήπους τέ σφισι καὶ τὸ βαλανεῖον τὸ ἐπώνυμον αὐτοῦ κατέλιπεν, ὥστε προῖκα αὐτοὺς λοῦσθαι, χωρία τινὰ ἐς τοῦτο τῷ Αὐγούστῳ δούς. καὶ ὃς οὐ μόνον ταῦτ' ἐδημιοίευσεν, ἀλλὰ καὶ καθ' ἑκατὸν δραχμὰς τῷ δήμῳ ὡς καὶ ἐκείνου κελεύσαντος διένειμε.

LV, 8, 3 (The Campus Agrippae, the Porticus Vipsania, the Diribitorium)

Τό τε πεδίον τὸ Ἀγρίππειον, πλὴν τῆς στοᾶς, καὶ τὸ διριβιτώριον αὐτὸς ὁ Αὔγουστος ἐδημοσίευσε. τοῦτο μὲν γάρ (ἦν δὲ οἶκος μέγιστος τῶν πώποτε μίαν ὀροφὴν σχόντων· νῦν γὰρ δὴ πάσης τῆς στέγης αὐτοῦ καθαιρεθείσης, ὅτι οὐκ ἠδυνήθη αὖθις συστῆναι, ἀχανὴς ἐστιν) ὅ τε Ἀγρίππας οἰκοδομούμενον κατέλιπε, καὶ τότε συνετελέσθη. ἡ δὲ ἐν τῷ πεδίῳ στοά, ἣν ἡ Πῶλλα ἡ ἀδελφὴ αὐτοῦ ἡ καὶ τοὺς δρόμους διακοσμήσασα ἐποίει, οὐδέπω ἐξείργαστο.

LXVI, 24 (The Saepta, the Basilica Neptuni, the Baths, the Pantheon, the Diribitorium)

Πῦρ δὲ δὴ ἕτερον ἐπίγειον τῷ ἑξῆς ἔτει πολλὰ πάνυ τῆς Ῥώμης, τοῦ Τίτου πρὸς τὸ πάθημα τὸ ἐν τῇ Καμπανίᾳ γενόμενον ἐκδημήσαντος, ἐπενείματο· καὶ γὰρ τὸ Σεραπεῖον καὶ τὸ Ἰσεῖον τά τε σέπτα καὶ τὸ Ποσειδώνιον τό τε βαλανεῖον τὸ τοῦ Ἀγρίππου καὶ τὸ Πάνθειον τό τε Διριβιτώριον καὶ τὸ τοῦ Βάλβου θέατρον καὶ τὴν τοῦ Πομπηίου σκηνήν, καὶ τὰ Ὀκταουίεια οἰκήματα μετὰ τῶν βιβλίων, τόν τε νεὼν τοῦ Διὸς τοῦ καπιτωλίου μετὰ τῶν συννάων αὐτοῦ κατέκαυσεν.

STRABO

II, 5, 17, C 120 (Agrippa's Map)

διὰ γὰρ τῶν τοιούτων ἤπειροί τε καὶ ἔθνη καὶ πόλεων θέσεις εὐφυεῖς ἐνενοήθησαν καὶ τἆλλα ποικίλματα, ὅσων μεστός ἐστιν ὁ χωρογραφικὸς πίναξ.

V, 3, 8, C 235–236 (The Sewers, the Aqueducts, Agrippa's other buildings, the Campus Agrippae)

οἱ δ' ὑπόνομοι συννόμῳ λίθῳ κατακαμφθέντες ὁδοὺς ἁμάξαις χόρτου πορευτὰς ἐνίας ἀπολελοίπασι. τοσοῦτον δ' ἐστὶ τὸ εἰσαγώγιμον ὕδωρ διὰ τῶν ὑδραγωγείων ὥστε ποταμοὺς διὰ τῆς πόλεως καὶ τῶν ὑπονόμων ῥεῖν, ἅπασαν δὲ οἰκίαν σχεδὸν δεξαμενὰς καὶ σίφωνας καὶ κρουνοὺς ἔχειν ἀφθόνους, ὧν πλείστην ἐπιμέλειαν ἐποιήσατο Μάρκος Ἀγρίππας, πολλοῖς καὶ ἄλλοις ἀναθήμασι κοσμήσας τὴν πόλιν. (Then follows a description of Rome, particularly of the Campus Martius.) *πλησίον δ' ἐστὶ τοῦ πεδίου τούτου καὶ ἄλλο πεδίον καὶ στοαὶ κύκλῳ παμπληθεῖς καὶ ἄλση καὶ θέατρα τρία καὶ ἀμφιθέατρον καὶ ναοὶ πολυτελεῖς καὶ συνεχεῖς ἀλλήλοις, ὡς πάρεργον ἂν δόξαιεν ἀποφαίνειν τὴν ἄλλην πόλιν.*

XIII, 1, 19, C 590 (Stagnum Agrippae, the Euripus, the Lion of Lysippus)

ἐντεῦθεν (*i.e.* from Lampsacus) *δὲ μετήνεγκεν Ἀγρίππας τὸν πεπτωκότα λέοντα, Λυσίππου ἔργον· ἀνέθηκε δὲ ἐν τῷ ἄλσει τῷ μεταξὺ τῆς λίμνης καὶ τοῦ εὐρίπου.*

2. Latin Sources

Pliny, *Nat. Hist.*

XXXVI, 102 (The Diribitorium)

Nec ut circum maximum a Caesare dictatore exstructum longitudine stadiorum trium, latitudine unius, sed cum aedificiis iugerum quaternum, ad sedem $\overline{\text{CCL}}$ inter magna opera dicamus, non inter magnifica basilicam Pauli columnis e Phrygibus mirabilem forumque divi Augusti et templum Pacis Vespasiani Imp. Aug. pulcherrima operum quae umquam vidit orbis, non et tectum diribitori ab Agrippa facti, cum theatrum ante texerit Romae Valerius Ostiensis architectus ludis Libonis?

XXXVI, 104-108 (The Sewers)

Sed tum senes aggeris vastum spatium, substructiones Capitolii mirabantur, praeterea cloacas, opus omnium dictu maximum subfossis montibus atque, ut paullo ante retulimus, urbe
pensili subterque navigata M. Agrippae in aedilitate post con-
105 sulatum. Permeant corrivati septem amnes ursuque prae-
cipiti torrentium modo rapere atque auferre omnia coacti, in-
super imbrium mole concitati vada ac latera quatiunt, aliquando
Tiberis retro infusus recipitur, pugnantque diversi aquarum
106 impetuus intus, et tamen obnixa firmitas resistit. Trahuntur
moles superne tantae non succumbentibus cavis operis, pulsant
ruinae sponte praecipites aut inpactae incendiis, quatitur solum
terrae motibus, durant tamen a Tarquinio Prisco annis DCC
prope inexpugnabiles, non omittendo memorabili exemplo vel
magis, quoniam celeberrimis rerum conditoribus omissum est.
107 Cum id opus Tarquinius Priscus plebis manibus faceret, es-
setque labor incertum maior an longior, passim conscita nece
Quiritibus taedium fugientibus, novom et inexcogitatum ante
posteaque remedium invenit ille rex ut omnium ita defunctorum
corpora figeret cruci spectanda simul civibus et feris volucribus-
108 que laceranda. Quamobrem pudor Romani nominis proprius,
qui saepe res perditas servavit in proeliis, tunc quoque subvenit,
sed illo tempore in post vitam erubescens, cum puderet vivos
tamquam puditurum esset extinctos. Amplitudinem cavis eam
fecisse proditur ut vehem faeni large onustam transmitteret.

XXXVI, 121 (The Aqueducts)

Q. Marcius Rex iussus a senatu aquarum Appiae, Anienis, Tepulae ductus reficere novam a nomine suo appellatam cuniculis per montes actis intra praeturae suae tempus adduxit, Agrippa vero in aedilitate adiecta Virgine aqua ceterisque conrivatis atque emendatis lacus DCC fecit, praeterea salientes D, castella CXXX, complura et cultu magnifica, operibus iis signa CCC aerea aut marmorea inposuit, columnas e marmore CCCC, eaque omnia annuo spatio. Adicit ipse aedilitatis suae conmemoratione et ludos diebus undesexaginta factos et gratuita praebita balinea CLXX, quae nunc Romae ad infinitum auxere numerum.

SUETONIUS, *Vit. Claud.* 18 (The Diribitorium)

Urbis annonaeque curam sollicitissime semper egit. Cum Aemiliana pertinacius arderent, in diribitorio duabus noctibus mansit ac deficiente militum ac familiarum turba auxilio plebem per magistratus ex omnibus vicis conuocavit ac positis ante se cum pecunia fiscis ad subueniendum hortatus est, repraesentans pro opera dignam cuique mercedem.

AELIUS SPARTIANUS, *Vit. Hadriani*, 19, 9-10 (Hadrian's Restorations)

Cum opera ubique infinita fecisset, numquam ipse nisi in Traiani patris templo nomen suum scripsit. Romae instauravit Pantheum, saepta, basilicam Neptuni, sacras aedes plurimas, forum Augusti, lavacrum Agrippae, eaque omnia propriis auctorum nominibus consecravit.

Curiosum and *Notitia* (Reg. VII and IX)

Curiosum

Regio VII. Via lata. Continet lacum Ganymedis. Cohortem I vigilum. Arcum novum. Nymfeum Iobis. Aedicula capraria. Campum Agrippae. Templum Solis et castra. Porticum Gypsiani et Constantini. Equos Tiridatis regis Armeniorum. Forum suarium. Mansuetas. Lapidem pertusum. Vici XV. Aedes XV. Vicomagistri XLVIII. Curatores II. Insulae $\overline{\text{III}}$DCCCV. Domus CXX. Horrea XXV. Balnea LXXV. Lacos LXXVI. Pistrina XVI. Continet pedes $\overline{\text{XIII}}$ CCC.

Notitia

Regio VII. Via lata. Continet lacum Ganymedis. Cohortem primam vigilum. Arcum novum. Nymfeum Iovis. Aediculam caprariam. Campum Agrippes. Templum Solis et castra. Porticum Gyptiani et Constantini. Templa duo nova Spei et Fortunae. Equum Tiridatis regis Armeniorum. Forum suarium. Hortos Largianos. Mansuetas. Lapidem pertusum. Vici XV. Aediculae XV. Vicomagistri XLVIII. Curatores II. Insulae $\overline{\text{III}}$DCCCV. Domos CXX. Horrea XXV. Balinea LXXV. Laci LXXVI. Pistrina XV. Continet pedes quindecim milia septingentos.

Curiosum

Regio VIIII. Circus Flaminius. Continet stabula IIII factionum VI. Porticum Philippi. Minuciam veterem et frumentariam. Cryptam Balbi. Theatra III. In primis Balbi, qui capet loca $\overline{XI}$.DX. Pompei capet loca $\overline{XVII}$.DLXXX. Marcelli capet loca $\overline{XX}$. Odium capet loca $\overline{X}$DC. Stadium capet loca $\overline{XXX}$. LXXXVIII. Campum Martium. Trigarium. Ciconias nixas. Pantheum. Basilicam Neptuni. Matidies. Marcianes. Templum Antonini et columnam coclidem altam pedes CLXXV S. gradus intus habet CCIII, fenestras LVI. Thermas Alexandrinas et Agrippianas. Porticum Argonautarum et Meleagri. Iseum et Serapeum. Minervam Calcidicam. Divorum. Insulam Felicles. Vici XXXV. Aedes XXXV. Vicomagistri XLVIII. Curatores II. Insulae $\overline{II}$DCCLXXVII. Domus CXL. Horrea XXV. Balnea LXIII. Lacos CXX. Pistrina XX. Continet pedes $\overline{XXXII}$D.

Notitia

Regio VIIII. Circus Flaminius. Continet stabula numero IIII, factionum VIII. Aedem Herculis. Porticum Philippi. Minucias duas, veterem et frumentariam. Cryptam Balbi. . Theatra tria, in primis Balbi, qui capit loca octo milia LXXXVIII, Marcelli capit loca $\overline{XVI}$DLXXX, . Pompei capit loca $\overline{XXII}$DLXXX. Odium capit loca $\overline{XI}$DX. Stadium capit loca $\overline{XXXIIII}$DCCCLXXXVIII. Campum Martium. Trigarium. Ciconias nixas. Pantheum. Basilicam Matidies. Martianes. Templum Divi Antonini et columnam coclidem altam pedes CLXXV semis, gradus intus habet CCIII, fenestras LVI. Hadrianium. Thermas Alexandrianas et Agrippianas. Porticum Argonautarum et Meleagri. Iseum et Serapeum. Divorum. Insulam Felicles. Vici XXXV. Aediculae XXXV. Vicomagistri XLVIII. Curatores II. Insulae $\overline{II}$DCCLXXVII. Domos CXL. Horrea XXV. Balinea LXIII. Lacos LXIII. Pristina XX. Continet pedes triginta duo milia quingentos.

INDEX

www.ingramcontent.com/pod-product-compliance
Lightning Source LLC
LaVergne TN
LVHW020651100826
845148LV00012B/2429